Tales of the Unexploded

A Rant Of Mediocre Proportion

By

Colin J Anderson

Tales of the Unexploded
Copyright © 2011 Colin J Anderson

First published 2011 by Lulu.com

2nd Edition. August 2011

ISBN:978-1-4478-2012-3

Acknowledgments

During the process of putting this book together I became aware that I would quite quickly become indebted to some people who had contributed either inadvertently or unexpectedly to the final outcome of this wonderful publication.

Some names that spring readily to mind are as follows: Michaela Anderson for the front cover photography. Scott Bailey for the back cover photograph. Marilyn Eckel on the island of St Maarten for her critique, a random German woman for the Drosselgasse photograph, Michael Anderson for providing welcome distractions from time to time, John Manuel on the island of Rhodes for some technical input regarding layouts etc. I should also thank the people of Great Britain who have provided enough annoyance for me to have the chance to rant and rage about many unnecessary things and send me well on the way to becoming a grumpy old man.

I also thank in anticipation the many friends of mine who have promised to buy this and read and cherish it forever and unabashedly promote it wherever and whenever they have the chance. I shall warmly remember you as all my royalties roll in and my bank balance swells by...ooh, tens of pounds. Thank you all. The stories contained in this journal are all true however unbelievable they may seem. My life actually is this bizarre/dull. Some brief events mentioned also have video evidence to confirm their authenticity and can be found by searching for "Tales of the Unexploded" on Youtube. Other events cannot be authenticated by any other means than by the scars on my body or a sad look in my eyes.

Finally my heartfelt thanks go out to the people who have inspired, encouraged, amused me and supplied me with unusual cheeses, pork pies with pickle built in (genius) and unexpected joy from time to time. You know who you are. And to all the people who thought this wasn't possible or wouldn't happen I warmly invite you to eat your words, or better still, buy this and eat mine.

Colin Anderson

CONTENTS

Day One – Page 14
A Brownie Point for Me

Day Two – Page 19
Cake 'O' Clock

Day Three – Page 24
Butt Naked from the Waist Down

Day Four – Page 30
The Actress & the Shopkeeper

Day Five – Page 37
Six Dead Bees

Day Six – Page 42
Omelettes & Logs

Day Seven – Page 46
"If You Didn't Have Bones, You'd Be Flat"

Day Eight – Page 51
A Leonberger

Day Nine – Page 55
A Social Scientist?

Day Ten – Page 60
"My God, Ziss Tastes Like Bleach"

Day Eleven – Page 64
Thank You Jeffrey Archer

Day Twelve – Page 69
An Electrode Each

Day Thirteen – Page 74
Funny Shaped Head

Day Fourteen – Page 80
1000 Sit-ups & Big Paul

Day Fifteen – Page 85
Special Panty Pads

Day Sixteen – Page 90
The Lovely Nigella

Day Seventeen – Page 96
Anon.

Day Eighteen – Page 101
Twenty To Four

Day Nineteen – Page 107
Sticky Knuckles

Day Twenty – Page 111
A Rash

Day Twenty One – Page 116
Farting On A Westie

Day Twenty Two – Page 120
"No Starters?"

Day Twenty Three – Page 127
Kissing David Bellamy

Day Twenty Four – Page 133
Hot Chocolate & A Tart

Day Twenty Five – Page 143
A Kid In Scotland

Day Twenty Six – Page 149
My Three Inch Floating Head

Day Twenty Seven – Page 155
Playing The Stick

Day Twenty Eight – Page 166
Mr Nix

Day Twenty Nine – Page 175
You Know Who Your Friends Are

Day Thirty – Page 181
Death In A Bottle

Conclusion – Page 186

Update On The April 2011 Legislation – Page 189

Recipes & Other Pointless Cookery Stuff – Page 190

Tales of the unexploded.

Obesity Chart.

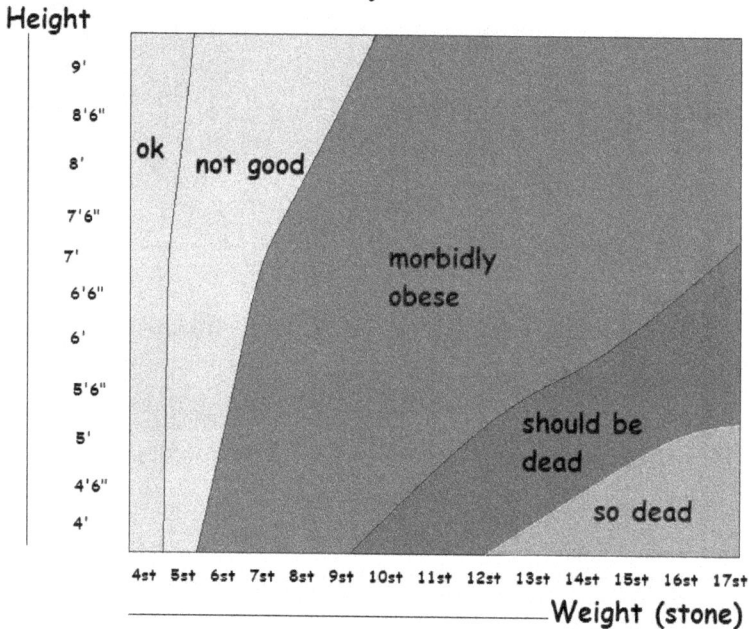

Height

9'
8'6"
8'   ok   not good
7'6"
7'
6'6"   morbidly
                          obese
6'
5'6"
5'   should be
                                dead
4'6"
4'   so dead

4st 5st 6st 7st 8st 9st 10st 11st 12st 13st 14st 15st 16st 17st

Weight (stone)

After a recent trip to the doctors and being told that I was morbidly obese (see chart, it should have been a pie chart but the doctor thought I'd eat it), and after reaching 41 years of age and deciding that I was fed up with my forehead slipping down over my eyes when I walked down the stairs, I felt the need to set myself the goal of losing some weight.

It's not about ego or making myself attractive to women or small animals but it's for my own sense of achievement and self esteem. At the end of the day, my friends already accept me for who I am, I've been married for over 20 years so my wife doesn't care if I'm Brad Pitt or Gordon Brown, just as long as I take the bins out on the right day of the

8

week and can open the lids of jars for her.

So, this challenge is a personal thing for me, although my kids would be over the moon if I could fit into a sack for the dads sack race at school sports day, rather than take my own custom made double sleeping bag.

So first of all, let me give you some idea of who I am and what my situation in life is: Like I said, I've reached the grand old age of 41, or as my son puts it, I have orbited the sun 41 times and to be honest, I've been in better shape. In my teens I was into cycling in a big way and even had the blood-restricting shorts that would make a maggot look like a python, they were so tight they plaited my bum hair, crikey, I even had matching gloves and aerodynamic glasses. It wasn't seen as particularly necessary to wear helmets back in those days, but I'm almost convinced that my '80s style permed quiff would have soaked up any concussions the speeding concrete roads could have thrown at me.

I was probably cycling 200-300 miles a week, I was playing badminton 2-3 times a week, swimming and doing weight training. As our American cousins might say, I was "awesome". I could eat what I wanted and drink what I wanted. I had a particular fondness for prawn cocktail crisps and I could easily get through twelve packets in one cycling trip. I don't know if it was the carbohydrates giving me a buzz or the skin tight shorts, but cycling and prawn cocktail crisps went together like sausage and mash, or rum and coke. The only down side was that when I pooped, I smelt like a harbour.

On the cycling trips other crisp flavours were sampled and I became quite the connoisseur. Round crisps, square crisps, tubes, oaty, crunchy, add your own salt and vinegar, and then someone made pyramid shaped crisps filled with cheddar cheese flavoured goo. Genius!! But I always returned to the prawn cocktail flavour as my favourite.

Happy days they were, munching, lunching and crunching. I have to say, I was royally upset when some clown decided to swap the colours of cheese and onion with salt and vinegar. Yes Mr crisp manufacturer, you know who you are!

I did all the usual things teens did in the '80s, listened to Howard Jones, Nik Kershaw, Modern Romance (hence the permed hair), played on my Atari 800xl and did the obligatory Youth Training Scheme where they taught me the ever useful skills of how to operate a Telex machine (which I was reliably informed they had on oil rigs!!)and how to type with one hand on some device that was apparently used in courtrooms or by pirates, that's if we weren't stuffing flyers into the local free newspaper for some grumpy Italian guy. But nevertheless, they paid me £27.50 a week and I thought I was king of the world.

Then out of the blue, a job came up in the Department of the Environment paying £60.00 per week! (testing my maths skills, I'd say that's nearly double!!), so I took the job and spent the next fourteen years or so moving around different government departments, doing a variety of jobs but mostly sitting on my ever increasing buttocks.

After many years of butt-kissing (other peoples, not my own, although technically by this time it wasn't impossible) and getting nowhere, I decided enough was enough and with the goading, sorry, I mean encouragement of my parents, I took the plunge and went self employed as a window cleaner.

The weight dropped off of me. I had gone from sitting down for nine hours a day, snacking on a drawer full of nibbles, pretzels, the ever faithful prawn cocktail crisps and fizzy drinks, to walking a few miles a day, drinking lots of water and just having a ten minute break for lunch. I went from eighteen stone down to fifteen stone in a matter of months.

I hadn't felt so fit and well for years, I was jumping over six foot fences and running like a gazelle across roofs, much to the annoyance of my new customers who thought I was on some illegal substance.

As time went on, the appeal of window cleaning wore off. People didn't pay, cold winters came and I lived in a particularly wet part of the U.K. at the time. You may have heard of it, it's a little place called Wales.

So then I trained as a pest controller, and that's mainly what I do to this day, although the recession has hit this business too and things have gone a little quiet, so once again I find myself snacking and piling on the pounds and reaching to the back of the wardrobe for my old "big" clothes, size 18 shirt collars and 38"waist trousers, although if I may clarify this a little, I am actually a 37" waist but they only seem to make trousers in a 36" or 38" which are unsurprisingly too tight or too loose.

Despite the doctors pronouncement of doom and instantaneous death on me, I don't agree that I am morbidly obese. I'm big boned. I know a lot of people laugh at that, but my father is the same. He has wrists the size of most people's necks. I'm 6'1" or 6'2" and can still see my bits when I pee, but doing my shoes up is becoming a bit of an excursion and my knees click like a bag of Lego when I bend down. So rather than do nothing about it, I'm going to set myself this thirty day goal and record the results, good or bad and throw in the odd story here and there from my life. Hopefully it will spur me on and be interesting for my children to read when I'm dead and gone, buried in a custom made bunker.

Maybe like me, you would be overjoyed to be able to jump off the bottom stair and not get slapped in the eyes with your man boobs (especially if you're a woman).

The rest of the book is laid out a day at a time with a blank page at the end of each day for you to write a food diary of what you have gorged on that day. Unless this turns out to be an e-book, in which case it's just as easy for you to get a pad and make your own record of your daily guzzlings. The point of this is to make me and also you, more aware of our food intake. I mean if someone asked you what you had eaten last Thursday, could you remember? At the end of the book are some recipes you might want to try.

When I was in the government departments, some bright spark came up with an acronym. It was SMART. Things that we did had to be Specific, Measurable, Achievable, Realistic and Time bound.

Using that acronym I would say that my specific goal is to try and lose weight or at the very least, to have a written record of what I eat so that I can analyse it and see where I need to tweak a few things. It's measurable by me standing on some reinforced scales, achievable? ....well, we will see. Realistic? I don't see why not. Time bound? I am giving myself 30 days.

I shall weigh first thing tomorrow morning and start my quest. Who knows where it may lead, perhaps I shall find a six pack in my shirt, to be honest though, I'd settle for a two pack. Lets try and keep this achievable and realistic. I read somewhere that disappointment can really mess up your resolve, so I think I won't weigh again until the end of the 30 days.

Most of the days, in fact all of the days will contain a comment on what I've had for breakfast, any mid morning snacks, lunchtime guzzlings, mid afternoon morsels (if they happen) and teatime details interlaced with anything that's on my mind that day or things I just need to get off my chest in a blatant rant.

I'm reliably informed by a friend from the eastern side of Britain, that "teatime" seems to be a West country/Welsh expression. I really don't know if that's true but they've never lied to me before. So perhaps I should clarify what I'm referring to.

Teatime for me has always been the meal that you eat (if you're lucky) at around 5pm, it generally consists of something cooked as opposed to cucumber sandwiches and a pot of earl grey tea. Nothing so refined will be taking place here. Maybe its just that more people tend to work through the day and have sandwiches at lunchtime and a cooked meal in the evening, but I do remember that teatime at my grandmothers was not a cooked meal. They would have perhaps a roast dinner at lunchtime and something lighter in the evening. This was their routine from when my grandfather retired. Previously when he was working, he would come home to a cooked meal and would take sandwiches for lunchtime in a small metal box that looked very much like a miniature bus shelter. It was light blue with the paint chipped off here and there. I don't know why I remember that or even why I mentioned it, but that's probably how this journal will unfold, randomly and for no good reason. You have been warned.

So going back to my point about "teatime", when I say this I mean it is the meal that happens at the end of the day and will generally be cooked unless there is a power cut or gas shortage. Now that's cleared up lets get on with this.

Day one - Monday- A brownie point for me.

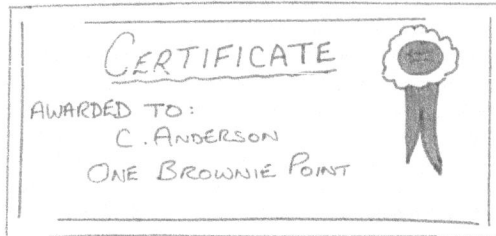

Breakfast:

OK, I've just weighed and to my surprise I'm exactly 18 stone, so that's a nice and easy place to start from although I'm not even on the chart at the start of this book. (which just to put your minds at rest, is a fictional chart created by me to highlight the stupidity of all the height/weight charts I have ever seen.)

Depending on what medical journal you might glance at in the doctors waiting room or what website you click on after you have Googled "fat man", you will be presented with a whole range of statistics and figures that all seem to point to the fact that if you are about six feet tall and over twelve stone, you are a human impossibility or perhaps a newly discovered planet.

I don't feel enormous or even obese but unfortunately I've woken up feeling less than positive and could murder a bacon and egg roll, however , instead I'm reaching for crunchy cereals and a cup of tea.

I expect the cereals are marinated in sugar and deep fried in cholesterol but given the alternatives and my limited time to prepare something that is stupendously healthy, these will do.

I'm using semi skimmed milk. I know skimmed would be better but I just cant stand it. Its like those paints you get, white with a hint of badger, city grey with a brief glimpse of countryside, you know the ones, well, skimmed milk is like water with a hint of cow or a whiff of udder.

Off to work now and taking two ham sandwiches, a bag of crisps and a banana. I've got into a habit of snacking in the middle of the morning as I'm working next to a bakery. Lets see if I can make it until lunchtime and resist the temptation, the lure of the smell of baking bread drifting through the air.

Lunchtime:

Well, I made it this far and didn't go near the bakery, so that's a brownie point for me. Aaaagh, I said brownie and now I'm thinking of chocolate fudge brownies dripping in hot chocolate sauce.

Tucking into the sandwiches now, its surprising how the taste of reformed pig can be improved by adding crisps to the sandwich. My banana has seen better days. Unbelievably it's a "fun size" banana. Maybe I'm missing the point, but I just haven't found the fun part yet. Thanks to the geniuses in Brussels this banana isn't even long enough to have any curvature to make it look like a smile. It just lays there looking enigmatic.

Right then, I need to focus on something else and not think about food. Tea time is only about four hours away. Feel like I haven't prepared very well for what I'm cautiously going to call a 'diet'. I need to have a bit of a think and try and get into the right frame of mind, otherwise this may not work out very well.

I've been thinking that maybe I should make a sort of smoothie, milkshake thing and "snack" on that through the day. I shall see what I have in the cupboard later and get a bit inventive.....maybe.

Years ago when I was trying to bulk up a bit I would make milkshakes from the weight gain powders you buy in sports shops and mix in raw eggs, two or three at a time. I'd also eat loads and loads of peanuts. The kids in school believed that I had a potentially fatal peanut allergy and so would make me play Russian roulette with a bag of Revels. It was actually a crafty way for me to eat a bag of Revels without sharing them.

The weight gain powders seemed to do what they were meant to do and I bulked up a bit. I must have been a bean pole because a year or two back I found my wedding suit in the back of the wardrobe and I couldn't even get my arms in the sleeves or the trousers over my thighs. Which was a shame as it was a tailor made suit, made from handmade Italian wool. I don't know what that means, whether some Italians combed the sheep themselves or what, but I do know it cost me a few months salary. The jacket cost nearly £500 and the trousers nearly £300, and that was twenty one years ago. I don't think I've been as extravagant since or ever will again but it fitted like a glove, which you would damn well expect at that price.

The fittings were an eye opener when I went to the tailors. The man measuring my various parts asked me which side I dressed on and I said "at the end of the bed usually". Apparently though it means which way your private parts lean towards and this has a bearing on how much extra material they stitch in. I like to tell myself that's why the trousers were so expensive. These days there's not so much of a dress side for me, more of a "it lands where it lands" attitude.

Teatime:

I've got quarter of a bacon quiche, some potato croquettes and some sweet corn for tea, washed down with a glass of squash.

Looking back at the first days food intake, I wouldn't say that I've particularly been a pig or exceeded any world records for food consumption. I think my main problem is in the evenings between having my tea and going to bed. I tend to wear a groove in the floor going back and fore to the larder and keep opening the fridge thinking that miraculously something tasty would have appeared in there since I last looked ten minutes ago.

Also a lack of exercise has added to my weight and also my general lethargy. Like I said earlier, I need get a bit more organised if I'm going to make this work.

Just a few hours to go before bed so I wonder if my wife could tie me down to the chair to keep me from going to the fridge, but I'm afraid to

16

ask her in case she gets the wrong idea. Mind you, after twenty years of marriage I don't think that will happen even if I wanted it to. I think I will get a pint of water though and sip on that through the evening to see if it distracts me enough to avoid snacking.

Day 1 - Your Food Diary

Breakfast

Mid Morning

Lunchtime

Teatime

Other snacks

Day 2 - Tuesday -Cake 'O' Clock.

Breakfast:

Right then, I'm not weighing today.
I am having a bowl of cereals that are apparently knitted by some old folk, drenched in semi skimmed milk, with a cup of tea.

I've also made a thick milkshake out of a diet powder that I'm going to take to work, I've mixed in some glucose powder to give it extra texture and to give me a bit of an energy boost. All that is shaken up with nearly a pint of semi skimmed milk. I'm hoping to sup on that through the day, or as long as it lasts. That should be a distraction and maybe take the edge off of any cravings. Usually about 11am my body is informing me that its cake 'o'clock and I feel an invisible force drawing me towards the bakery or failing that, back to bed.

Talking of bed, we bought a memory foam mattress recently and I have to say it takes some getting used to. Within seconds of you laying on it, the lower part of your body that is in contact with the mattress disappears and you look a bit like a muffin oozing out of a cake tin. This morning when I put my foot on the bed to put on a sock, I wasn't as quick as I should have been and I watched in bemused silence as my foot sank out of view into the depths of the memory foam. I eventually got my foot back minus the sock. Maybe it will turn up one day and hopefully I will have no more clothes related incidents today.

Mid-morning

What a morning! A whole procession of people have come in asking for things that just don't make sense. I really couldn't make this stuff up if I tried, it's not even funny. Here's an example, a lady came in this morning and said "someone's put me on a tablet and I wondered if you sold it".
Then she looked at me expecting me to know exactly what she was on about and what specific tablet out of the zillion or so available that she needed.

"Who put you on this tablet?", I said, "your doctor?".

"No someone at school". The fact she was in her fifties and most definitely not at school didn't seem to make any difference.

"OK", I said, "It would help if you knew what it was called". And this is the bit I couldn't make up and wouldn't make up as it's just so weird, "I think its called radio flute" she said!!!

"That's not one I'm familiar with" I said, resisting the urge to slap her with a large plank, "What's it for?"

"I'm going in for an operation and it helps you to heal quicker"

This is the short version but what she actually wanted was Arnica tablets. Unbelievable. This happens from time to time but you never get used to it. Never mind, it's lunchtime soon.

Lunchtime:

Well, here we are and once again I didn't head to the bakers. The milkshake idea was a good one, although the real idea is that the milkshake replaces one of your meals (according to the manufacturer). I'm not sure I could go with that. I'm almost certain that I would black out or at least be majorly grumpy if I didn't have some kind of solid food for lunch. It really does affect my mood if I'm hungry. I can go from being jovial and happy to evil and murderous in the blink of a Battenberg.

20

So in addition to the milkshake (which I have almost finished) I am having 2 ham sandwiches with mustard, a bag of crisps and an enigmatic banana again.

The milkshake has filled me up so I'm hoping the afternoon will pass by without the usual pangs of "hunger". I say "hunger" in quotation marks because we don't know we are born in the western world do we? There's children starving in the world who would give anything just to have a tenth of what we eat here or even to have what we waste. Generally I think I don't waste too much and in some ways this has contributed to my balloon-like appearance, for example if my son doesn't finish his tea, I can't throw it out so I will eat it, which is a bit like having another small meal every day. If you add that up over a period of time it's not an insignificant pile of food.

Teatime:

Aha, my wife has made spaghetti bolognaise for tea with garlic bread. I'm not even going to ask her if it's a 'light' sauce, I shall just sit in silence and eat while the kids relay all the grizzly goings on of their day at school. It's always fun to watch my son slurping in spaghetti. I never cease to be amazed at how a kid can get bolognaise sauce, or any other sauce for that matter behind their ears or on the back of their head or on the wall behind them. It defies all logic.

Snack time:

OK, well the evening is here and I'm faced with a few snacky options. Some Japanese rice crackers and a Martini, or an apple. Oh dammit, I'm going for the apple. Do you know what? It actually filled me up a bit.

Once again I would say that I haven't exceeded any records or broken any local laws regarding food consumption today. I haven't really done what you would class as a physical job today though. From time to time there's some lifting of stock, like sacks of sunflower seeds or mixed nuts, but generally I'm standing in one of about three places, at the till, by the shelves advising customers or in the kitchen area, bagging up new stock. If I can get my head around it, I should try and devise some sort of exercise that I can incorporate into my daily routine without bursting a blood vessel.

Right, I'm off to bed before the voices from the fridge get any louder.

Day 2 - Your Food Diary

Breakfast

Mid Morning

Lunchtime

Teatime

Other snacks

Day 3 - Wednesday - Butt naked from the waist down.

Breakfast:

I'm sticking with the wheaty knitted breakfast and a cup of tea as it seems to keep me fairly well filled up until nearly lunchtime. Here's something ironic I forgot to mention to you but hinted at yesterday when I said about carrying sacks of sunflower seeds etc. My parents have set up and run their own health shop for over 20 years, and while my work as a pest controller has gone a bit quiet, I'm working there at the moment. Only part time, but it gives me a small income, and it gives them a few opportunities to have a day off here and there. That's the plan anyway.

Now, it would be fair to say that my parents have become…er, how can I put this, what you would call thick set and not the tanned and toned Adonis and Venus that you would want to see in a health shop, so in fact I fit right into the image that they have portrayed for so many years. Maybe sales will go up if I do lose a bit of weight.

Mid-morning:

Had a bit of a low morning so far and at about 11am decided it was cake 'O'clock so I went to the bakery next door and got a macaroon. I love macaroons, and if I'm not mistaken they are made with almonds, which is probably a fruit (yes ,yes, I know), so possibly it could be counted as one of my five a day. That theory suits me right now, so I'm sticking with it.

Actually, who the heck came up with the five a day thing? Is it some obscure government department? You'd be amazed at how many departments there are for doing stupid things, like the department of cow tipping, or the department of vegetable length calibration, or the department of navel fluff collection that checks to see what the average production figures are. I'm surprised they don't make us recycle it already to use as loft insulation or padding for cheap coats. Why is navel fluff always blue, or is that just me?

During my time in the Civil Service you wouldn't believe how many dull and pointless meetings I sat through. Talk about a waste of your life. And yet they would set up committees to assess certain facts and figures and then have a meeting to discuss the results. Some butt kissing would-be politician type would stand next to a white board and in a particularly irritating voice come out with something like "we have carefully gone over all the available data and correlated it with previous information that we already had from last years meetings, and we can say with some degree of certainty that the amount of monthly meetings we will be having within the next year will probably be around the eleven or twelve mark."

The presenter of this pointless tat, would then sit amongst other pointless tat-makers being heartily slapped on the back and they would all congratulate themselves on their awesome abilities. Unfortunately, these people are the ones that progressed to the higher echelons of the Civil Service to make up things like the "five a day" rule whilst what I call the more normal people usually left to set up their own businesses or do something a bit more useful like painting lines on the road.

My local council,which is no doubt chock-full of these high powered decision makers has just issued a whole new set of bins for us to divide our waste into. I am shocked or possibly stunned that there is no bin for the aforementioned navel fluff. Perhaps there has been some typing error and the bins for "Naval" fluff have been sent to the navy.

Anyway, like I said, a low morning. Just feeling a bit glum and hacked off with life at the moment, no particular incident has set this off, just a general feeling of malaise that has crept up on me and tried to bite me in the bum.

Looking on the bright side though, it will soon be lunchtime.

Lunchtime:

I didn't make sandwiches today, just crusty rolls, two of them, filled with ham, cheese and a spicy relish which appeared to be running for its life as I took a big bite and squirted it down the front of my white shirt. I now look like I've been lending a hand at a road traffic accident. I also have a bag of crisps, a chocolate biscuit and a banana. These crusty rolls aren't very easy to eat cleanly either. They shatter with every bite in much the same way I imagine a windscreen would if you could take a bite.

I will probably save the banana for later, it doesn't look too appetising anyway, sort of like a toy canoe with jaundice. I seem to remember as a child that bananas were much longer and more yellow and just looked an altogether more happy fruit.

Mid afternoon:

I had the banana. Wish I hadn't, it was what I can only describe as....dry. If that makes sense. As I ate it, it seemed to absorb any moisture from my mouth and throat and left me coughing like a two hundred year old smoker. I needed a big mug of water after that, which isn't necessarily a bad thing. I definitely don't drink enough water, I just find it so bland and the water here is so hard. After 20 years of lovely soft water in Wales, returning to the hard, lime scale laden water of the West country is a bit of a shock to my delicate, nearly girly palate.

Teatime:

Breaded fish, oven chips and peas. Never my favourite thing, fish. Without fail I always get a bone or twenty in my fish. I could go to the poshest restaurant in the world and order the No-boned boneless fish and still get a mouthful of bones, I seem to be a bone magnet. I'm surprised I never had bones in my prawn cocktail crisps.

So, as you may have guessed, I found some bones in this fish too. For that reason I always start with the fish, just in case I swallow some of the bones, I will have the rest of the meal to push them down my scratched and bone laden throat. I often imagine the inside of my throat looking like a rather macabre game of Ker-plunk after I've had fish. Lashings of red sauce make the whole experience bearable and also makes it easier to eat the peas as they all cling together.

Mid evening:

Had a cup of tea and some biscuits. Trying not to drink too late as I seem to be getting up about 1:00 am for a wee. I understand that's just something that comes with age too. Wondering if I could just set up some sort of guttering system around the edge of the bed, but then in my half-awake state I might face the wrong way and tsunami the wife out of bed.

This whole wee situation makes the prostate thing rear its ugly head, not literally, that would just look wrong and I'm not even sure it has anything resembling a head. But I read somewhere that when a man has to pee in the night, it can be a sign that there's some prostate problems looming on the horizon, and recently my grandfather has had treatment for that very thing. I did go and have my prostate checked a few years ago. Not a pleasant experience unless you're into that sort of thing.

There I was laying on my side, butt naked from the waste down except for my socks, with an extremely hairy doctor sitting so close to my backside that I could feel his breath on bits that should never feel breath let alone see the light of day. Then I heard the "thwack" of latex gloves being....well, thwacked and plunged into lard and the doctor offering those ever so helpful words "try and relax".

27

Seconds later my inner space was invaded and as deep as his fingers went in, my eyeballs exited equal distance the other end. I don't know if its something they teach them in medical school but just as I wasn't expecting it, he threw in the question "got any holidays planned this year?"

I don't remember my exact reply, but I think I said something through gritted teeth about not going pot-holing.

After a few more bizarre and untimely questions about my holiday plans and asking me if I liked gladiator films, I heard and felt the "thwop" of him returning his hand to the daylight and then after he had put my eyeballs back in their sockets and retrieved his watch from my orifice, he said that there was nothing unusual up there.

A little confused, I asked what he meant by unusual, had he expected to find loose change, abandoned shopping trolleys or out of season chutney's?

He explained that if there was any abnormal swelling, he would have felt that. It's the swelling that puts pressure on some part of your inner pee workings (please note and admire the use of medical terminology here) and slows the flow of your pee, so you never feel quite like you've finished.

So the short version of this is that I don't think I have prostate problems at this stage of my life, but that I may just be drinking too much fluid before I go to bed.

Right then, beddy byes.(you tend to say stupid things like that when you've got kids).

Day 3 - Your Food Diary

Breakfast

Mid Morning

Lunchtime

Teatime

Other snacks

Day 4 - Thursday – The Actress & the Shopkeeper.

Breakfast:

Hurrah! didn't pee until 6:30am
Forgot to get out of bed though! Darn it.

I've woken up late and haven't got time for breakfast. Have a quick cup
of tea though and grab a biscuit. Not sure what knock-on effect this will
have later in the day but I shall try and remain focused and positive
….nah, can't see that happening.

Mid morning:

Well, it's mid morning and I'm pretty hungry, so I've opted for a
flapjack bar, purchased from my very own parents health shop. It does
make me laugh that people assume if they get a snack from the health
shop it's going to be good for them. A big seller is yoghurt coated
raisins, people go on about it being fruit and one of their "5 a day", ha
ha, what about the sugar laden yoghurt "flavoured" coating? There's
about 4 zillion calories in one of them. I have to say though, the
yoghurt coated orange peel is delicious, its so strange but it just brings a
smile to your face. It's funny how food can do that.

I've got a friend who has a pretty depressing life but when you talk to
her about food, her eyes just light up in the way a stained glass window
floods the air with colour and gets so engrossed and excited telling you
about all the juicy details of tasty things she's tried, It's lovely to see
and she's a joy to be around when she's like that. If I was a millionaire I
would buy her a Deli just to see her smile. That's the power of good
food.

Just have a quick check of the calories in this flapjack…. Blimey, I shouldn't have looked, I'm still counting the zero's, there's almost a million calories in this bar. I don't even think Stephen Hawking could count these calories.

Its actually quite unhealthy, but I've paid for it now and unwrapped it so I shall have to do the decent thing and give it the attention it deserves.

Getting a bit distracted now as a man has just run at top speed past the window carrying what I think is called a "clapper board", you know the thing they snap shut when they start filming to synchronise sound and video. One of those. Maybe he's stolen it and is making his get-away.

Next I see an old man, probably in his eighties being "escorted" quicker than his frail legs can naturally go by a tall gentleman clutching a clipboard under his arm whilst aiding the old gentleman's bullet-like exit from the scene, almost lifting his feet off the ground.

Then, in this bizarre procession I see three men pulling something looking like a moon buggy with a man sitting on it aiming a very, very expensive camera down the road and there looking all neat and tidy is the subject of the cameraman's aim, the actress Anna Friel.

She walks along the pavement, turns and looks across the road and steps out into the traffic which is slowing down for the traffic lights. She crosses and passes near a group of elderly ladies waiting at the bus stop. They catch sight of the camera and start waving and Yoo-Hooing.

"Oh for god's sake, CUT" shouts the director into a walkie talkie, deafening most of the crew wearing ear-pieces. "Reset, let's go again!"

This process happens about twelve more times until the elderly hooligans are moved on by a security man who I think was known as Bomber, a large but quiet gentleman who got things sorted. He may have been quiet and kind faced but you just knew he could snap your neck with a twitch of his powerful biceps.

After getting the shot they wanted, the crew moved down the road a bit and started setting up their next scene. While this was being done, the actress crossed back over the road and came into the shop.

"Hello" she said cheerily.

"Miss Friel" I acknowledged, thinking I was as cool as ice cream and then turned and knocked everything off of the counter. Now I would never have thought I could be star struck, but Miss Friel induced a certain giddiness about me that lasted for quite some hours after her departure. I think my brain had trouble computing the fact that someone I had seen on the TV was here in person talking to me in real life. I must have had a little meltdown. Oh, and she is gorgeous.

When I picked up the items I had scattered and steadied myself against the counter, she asked a few questions about what would be good for a sore throat. I mumbled a few unintelligible sentences and then managed to ask if she would mind having a photograph taken with me, I mean after all it's not every day she gets to have her picture taken with a shopkeeper is it?

I took the photograph, totted up the cost of the goods she had bought and waved her goodbye. It wasn't until some time later when my brain had settled down that I realised I had short-changed her. So if you ever see Anna Friel, Hollywood actress and British national treasure, please tell her I'm sorry and that I owe her eighteen pence.

I do have the photograph and I was going to put it right here, but I just don't understand all the copyright laws. As I am the one that took the photo', I know I own the copyright, but as the actress is also in the photograph, we start getting into joint copyright. So, rather than get sued, as I'm already skint, I shall insert a picture of my son when he was little.

There's no good reason for this photograph to be here other than it saves me getting into trouble and I always liked the look on his face, and I still can't decide if it could be described as a look of disdain or mistrust. See what you think.

Can you see what I mean? What a face.

Maybe he thought I was going to take away his plastic octopus and deep fry it in batter. That's got me thinking about food again now. I've never had octopus. The nearest I came to it was tricking my daughter into eating squid by telling her it was onion rings. So not actually that near then.

Lunchtime:

As you will notice, I got up late and so I didn't have time to prepare something for lunch. Now I have the dilemma of making a choice. I could visit one of the two local bakeries or one of the three supermarkets. I feel I need something hot, don't know why, its not a particularly cold day but that's just what I fancy right now.

Hot in a bakery usually means a pasty or a pie and hot in a supermarket means something instant with hot water added. Decisions, decisions. Right then, I opted for the supermarket and I've come back with a pot of noodles which I am reliably informed is from Bombay and apparently it's a very bad boy. So, on goes the kettle, filling the pot to the line and adding a little packet of "flavour". Don't really understand the point of packaging the flavour separately. If I just wanted plain noodles I would have bought plain noodles or picked them myself from the noodle tree or wherever they come from.

This noodle snack was meant to be spicy but I haven't been able to detect that yet. I'm wondering if my taste buds have been destroyed by the chemicals they used to put in the prawn cocktail crisps I was so fond of. The strange thing is that I was never keen on the actual dish of prawn cocktail, and it doesn't seem too long ago that restaurants only had that and melon balls or soup on their starter menus. Thank goodness times have moved on and you can have breaded mushrooms with a garlic dip now.

I've decided there's nothing wrong with my taste buds, but something seriously wrong with my father's. We made a cup of tea just now and I went to pour in the milk but got a whiff of sourness. A more thorough sniffing revealed that the milk is going off. My dad doesn't seem to mind and has opted to have a sour cup of tea complete with floating lumpy bits. Me? I'm off to the shops to get some fresh milk. I'm a delicate soul.

Teatime:

I don't know what its called but its made up of mash with onion and bacon in it, mixed up with baked beans. Quite filling and nice to have the different textures all together. The recipe is at the back under the heading "mash thing". Pint of squash to wash it down.

Evening:

Well, surprisingly I have managed to get through the evening without too much temptation or snacking. I have to say that is largely down to the fact that I keep repeating, with a kind of semi burp-hiccup, the noodles I had earlier. Now I would say that is value for money. I'm not helping myself though by sitting and watching the food channel.

I've now got the crazy urge to roast a duckling, stuff a goose or wrap a haddock in Parma ham. I think it will be safer if I go to bed and leave all these foody shenanigans to the professionals.

Day 4 - Your Food Diary

Breakfast

Mid Morning

Lunchtime

Teatime

Other snacks

Day 5 - Friday – Six Dead Bees.

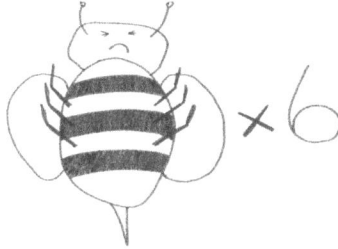

Breakfast:

Cereals for breakfast and a cup of tea. My nose has erupted in a mass of white heads!! Haven't got a clue what's brought it on but my face looks like a smacked backside and I can't even blame it on the "detox" effect of this diet because so far this isn't a diet, is it? Don't really feel like advising people on a healthy lifestyle today when I look like one of the experiments from the movie The Fly.

It's strange how acne can still take a forty one year old by surprise, usually with a huge pus filled gift just before an important occasion like a wedding or family reunion where a myriad photographs will be taken, forever immortalising the Siamese twin growing out of your nose.

I always dreaded P.E. at school as the teacher found great pleasure in humiliating the spotty boys in the class by giving lovely clean red tabards to the boys who already looked like aftershave models and sending them to one end of the gym, and then telling the rest of the acne gang to take off their tops as we were going to be "skins" at the other end of the gym.

We all knew he was being a ******* because there was a huge pile of unused blue tabards that would have quite easily identified us as a different team from the reds, apart from the already blatantly obvious gene-pool lottery results.

As it turned out, we sort of had the last laugh really, because as the game of football or tag rugby wore on, the more collisions we had, the

37

more spots were bursting and seeping and oozing, so we almost ended up wearing the red tabards anyway. Shower time after the game always looked like an explosion in a jam factory.

As the terms and school years wore on, our confidence grew and our level of being ticked off at the teacher grew almost as much as our spots, so we would always try and involve him in one or more of the collisions and manage to shed a few pounds of organic matter somewhere on him. In time, either the law changed or he got the message that "skins" wasn't such a good idea... which was a shame really as we had a mixed sex school.

Mid morning:

Strangely un-hungry at the moment and a little confused. Had a woman come in this morning asking if we knew a local bee keeper. As it happens, we do, but we thought she was trying to cut out the middle man (us) and get cheaper honey, but she wasn't.

She then asked if we wanted six dead bees.

We politely declined. She continued and told us that she had been out walking and found six dead bees and thought that she should warn a local bee keeper that there may be some bee virus on the loose.

I'm tempted to file this incident away in a pigeon-hole in my brain labelled "what the hell just happened?" but unfortunately there's some vague truth in what she's saying. It appears that there is something killing off the bees in the world, which at first glance doesn't seem like a problem and may even seem like a good thing if you are planning a picnic. But when you stop and think that most crops are pollinated by bees, if they aren't around, the crops won't grow. If the crops don't grow you're well on the way to having food shortages. So just a thought but, if you see a bee where it shouldn't be, don't kill it, just put it outside.

Lunchtime:

I didn't bring any lunch today and at the moment I'm still not feeling too hungry, but I guess if I don't get something to eat, I will snack like a lunatic later. So a quick wander to the supermarket gets me a pasta salad with chicken and peppers. Reduced price as well because the date is up today. Oh well, it won't poison me and I saved nearly a quid, that's one pound Sterling if you're outside the UK.

Actually it's not bad. Smothered in mayonnaise and sort of slimy. I don't even need to chew it as the pasta just skates from my lips to my throat on a pond of diluted mayo' & saliva. See? I could be a food critic for some real classy up-market publication.

The more of this I have, the more I feel a warm acidic burning in my chest. How strange. It almost tastes like some of the vinaigrette dressing has gone a bit rancid or something. Haven't got the inclination or time to take it back so I will just have to grimace and bear it.

Mid afternoon:

Having a cup of tea but the pasta keeps repeating on me. Another one of those value for money moments.

What a weird day, had a woman come in and say "my little one is suffering and not sleeping too well, she's three years old", turns out the little one is a cat. I'm not really a cat person, I just don't see the point in feeding an animal that never stays with you, doesn't protect you and costs you money. That's just like making packed lunches for your ex wife. Eh? That made sense when I first thought of it. My aversion to cats isn't helped by the fact that if I ever plant seeds in the garden, onions, cabbages, sprouts, carrots or whatever they may be, the whole cat population for a fifty mile radius decide to descend on my freshly dug patch and poop in it.

Oh well, the California poppy tincture should help with the cats insomnia.

Teatime:

OK, pasta for tea. Is that allowed? Pasta twice in one day? I guess it depends who you ask. My wife seems to think that I will get some terrible disease or food poisoning if I have more than one egg a day!! What about if I make an omelette? Hmm speaking of which I might do that tomorrow as its Saturday.

So, back to my tea, its pasta and chicken strips in a tomato sauce that's been cooked in the oven. Not my favourite as the pasta gets burnt and crunchy. Never mind, I'm too tired and polite to complain or make something else. I shall leave the complaining to the kids who seem to have no qualms in voicing their disgust when unusual or incinerated items are served up.

Day 5 - Your Food Diary

Breakfast

Mid Morning

Lunchtime

Teatime

Other snacks

Day 6 -Saturday - Omelettes and Logs

Breakfast:

Hooray, I had a lie in today. Funny how my kids are immune to weekends and haven't yet discovered the sheer joy of not getting up at the crack of dawn. For my daughter I think it's more a question of habit, she gets up early through the week for school and so even though she's tired at the weekends, her body clock is yelling at her to get up.

I need to potter around in the garden so I might make that omelette that I was thinking of yesterday. I'm not going to make it yet, I shall wait a bit so that I appreciate it more when I'm really hungry; but I will have a cup of tea. You shouldn't start the day without one. That's the law.

Mid morning:

I've been sorting out some wood and logs in the garden as we've just had a wood burning fire fitted. Just as well as all the prices for gas and electric are shooting up. Its been on the cards for a while so about three years ago I cut up some logs and put them in the greenhouse to season, which for those of you reliant on your new-fangled gas central heating, just means to "dry out". If you burn unseasoned or "wet" wood it tends to leave tarry deposits in the chimney lining, or to use an expression I heard somewhere, it will "clag" it up.

I recently purchased something called a log grenade, but much to my sons disappointment it wasn't the explosive device he had expected to see. It's a wedge of metal that you pound into the top of a log to split it. I have to say for such a simple device, it's been most effective this morning and made mincemeat of the logs, unlike my axe which is as much use as half a bag of spit.

So here I go with the omelette, looking forward to this as I didn't have any breakfast. During my window cleaning years I frequented a few very dodgy cafés and mobile eateries and something that always turned my stomach a bit was having a watery omelette. Now, I'm no chef but as far as my limited experiments have shown, its because too much milk has been used, so when I make an omelette, I just add a splash of milk or sometimes none at all and use at least 4 eggs. The recipe is at the end of the book.

Oh yum, that was good, very good, ten out of ten and the kids loved it as well and appreciated the fact that it wasn't swimming around their plates like a drowning UFO. I used to get Spanish omelette baguettes from a little sandwich shop up a side road off Westgate Street in Cardiff twenty years ago, and I can still taste it now. I don't know how the man made them but the whole thing was a meal in itself and was about £1.20. I feel a trip to Cardiff coming on just to see if that place is still there.

That was so filling that I'm not sure I feel like any lunch but that could change as I get physical with another tree trunk which I have to turn into chunks that will fit into my wood burner.

Lunchtime:

Well, as expected the omelette kept me going for a while and I am a little disinclined to indulge in the usual mid-day culinary frivolities. Basically I'm saying I'm not having lunch. I'm too full, but I will have a cup of tea and stop talking weird like that.

It's not usual for me to miss lunch, but today is a bit of a messed up day and I need to get this wood sorted out. A friend of ours planted a cherry tree about thirty years ago and it had grown with a branch hanging dangerously over the neighbours garden and needed to be taken down. That's what the majority of this wood is from. It's got a lovely colour and smell to it as I've been splitting it into bits.

I am however, having a pint of weak squash, just to lubricate me and to replenish my armpits which have been working overtime.

Teatime:

Hungry now but also tired from lumberjack activities. My wife doesn't feel up to making something and neither do I, so I think it will have to be something from the local takeaway. Thank goodness they do delivery.

Yes, it's not really in line with my "diet" but I have burnt more calories than usual today and I wouldn't want my body to go into shock or something. That would just be pointless and could set me back weeks or even years.

Do you see how I keep coming up with reasons to eat? I guess its just an inbuilt mechanism so that I don't starve. Maybe there's some less fattening options on the menu, lets have a look. Hmm, boiled rice instead of fried rice, not so tasty though is it? Vegetable curry, or chicken curry? I always find the vegetable curry makes me gassy so I should go for the chicken, with chicken fried rice, some chips and sweet and sour chicken balls. I would like to point out that this does get divided between all of us, its not just a pile of food for me.

A quick phone call and twenty minutes later, there's the doorbell with the delivery, time to divvy up the food and chill out watching some singing contest where the best singers get sent home and the freaks and weirdo's seem to prosper while the judges grin their far too white teethy smiles and congratulate themselves on how wonderful they are.

Quality entertainment. Quality food. A comfortable chair for my aching bones. What more could I want for?

Day 6 - Your Food Diary

Breakfast

Mid Morning

Lunchtime

Teatime

Other snacks

Day 7 -Sunday- "If you didn't have bones, you'd be flat."

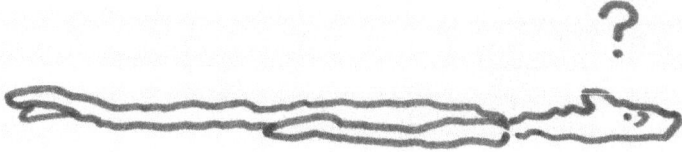

A lazy start to the day and I've woken up with a bad feeling. There is nothing particular that I can say has made me feel this way again, but I've woken up and feel like I should expect the worst. Mind you, I've exercised this theory for a long time that if you expect the worst and it doesn't happen, then you've probably had a good day. Maybe that makes me a Dismalist, but it works.

I seem to go into a coma during the early hours and my best sleep is between 4am and 9am. All sorts of things usually happen around me and over me. For example my wife will sometimes wash her hair in the shower and then have the hair-dryer on hurricane force whilst sitting at the end of my bed. I never hear it!

Sometimes my son comes in and jumps all over the bed and me. As long as he avoids delicate organs and doesn't land on any fleshy appendages, I don't wake up.

Its funny the things he notices and thinks about. A month or two back while sitting at the table eating our evening meal, I could see that he was looking me up and down and deep in thought. Then after a while he said "Dad, if you didn't have bones, you'd be flat."

How true.

Anyway, once again I have been in a coma-like state and now have woken to find that it is raining very heavily. Aah, it makes me feel like I'm back home in Wales, all I need is the sound of sheep bleating on the hills and the squeal of stolen cars racing around the streets. Bliss.

46

Actually, talking of sheep, we are having roast lamb for lunch today. I hope it lives up to my expectations, I always seem to be disappointed when we have lamb, either because it's way too fatty or far too chewy. Only once did I have a nice bit of lamb and that was in a Harvester restaurant in Pencoed, near Bridgend in Wales. Mint sauce just added that lovely finishing touch to it, yum yum.

Breakfast:

So, here we are again at the start of another day and I'm faced with the choice of making porridge or going for the easy cereal option. Yes, cereals it is, although looking deeper into the cupboard I see that I have some Goji berries to use up, so a quick change of plan and I'm now reaching for the porridge oats. I suppose that's a healthier option apart from the fact that I mix sugar into the warm milk and then when it's in the bowl I sprinkle more sugar on top and sometimes golden syrup. Let's see if I can cut down on the sugar. The Goji berries add a bit of sweetness and they're meant to be one of these "super foods", whatever that means. Surely all food has good attributes, OK, not the processed foods and burgers and breads and instant foods, but I mean all fruit, or berries, or vegetables. I shan't worry too much about it, I shall leave that to those who are paid to sit and wonder about nutrition.

Having made the porridge with the Goji's in, it's not bad. I might bear that in mind for another day. All I did was sprinkle a handful of them in halfway through making the porridge. Easy peasy breakfast with a cup of tea. The sort of breakfast you could easily prepare when camping. Some people though seem determined to make things more difficult than necessary when out and about.

There's no need to fanny around with too many pots or pans sometimes. Here's an example. Once I had to drive somewhere, where I'd been or where I was going is not important. The crucial thing here is to know that I'd been driving for about an hour and my engine was hot.

At the beginning of this journey I had filled a flask with boiling water, packed a spoon, a knife and fork, a packet of couscous and a bowl. The other important ingredient was a tuna steak in a foil container which I wedged into a gap next to the engine.

When I arrived at my destination, hey presto, a quick splash of hot water onto the couscous and open the now very hot packet of tuna and put it into the bowl. A simple tasty meal with very little effort. Cheap too.

I did this once in a car park when I was caught up in a bit of a traffic jam, I had the bonnet up and the engine running and a few people came to ask if everything was all right, had I broken down or something and why was I staring into the engine compartment. I explained that I hadn't broken down but that I was just preparing a tuna steak for my lunch. They looked at me like I had something bad written on my forehead and left me to my tuna steak in sweet chilli sauce.

More people should cook this way. My grandfather used to get a magazine in the 1950's from America, I think it was called Popular Mechanics. Somewhere I've got a faded copy and the adverts in there are fascinating, I mean some are bizarre but some are really good ideas. One that stuck in my mind and got me thinking about cooking on the car engine was the "Engine kitchen mate", it was like a metal tray with different compartments for various foods and it fitted onto the top of the engine of one of those big 1950's American cars.

If you Google "cooking on your car engine" or go onto Youtube, you will find lots of useful information. Not only are you getting good use out of otherwise wasted energy, but it's ruddy hilarious too, especially seeing the look of disbelief on peoples faces when they find out what you're doing.

The only down side is that your car might smell of sausages or Cajun prawns although it's a darn site better than dead mole. Trust me, I caught a mole one hot summer and put it in a bag in my van and then forgot about it for a few days. It took weeks to get rid of the stench and the maggots, so the smell of some meat cooking merrily away as you drive along shouldn't be a problem. Quite pleasant in fact.

Lunchtime:

Roast lamb, roast potatoes, Yorkshire puddings, green beans, carrots and gravy, with of course, mint sauce. Need I say anything else?
As for the lamb.....once again too fatty, but a really good flavour.
I need to have a lie down now, I've got that Sunday afternoon feeling. I don't know if it's in my genes or a habit from my childhood but there's a definite feeling of calm in the air on a Sunday afternoon that shouldn't be ignored. It should be savoured and grasped with both hands because Monday's coming and it ain't pretty.

Teatime:

That was a huge roast meal we had earlier and so I'm still a bit full and lethargic but decided to have lamb sandwiches and a cup of tea and try and chill out before the drudgery of the week begins tomorrow.

Day 7- Your Food Diary

Breakfast

Mid Morning

Lunchtime

Teatime

Other snacks

50

Day 8 - Monday - A Leonberger.

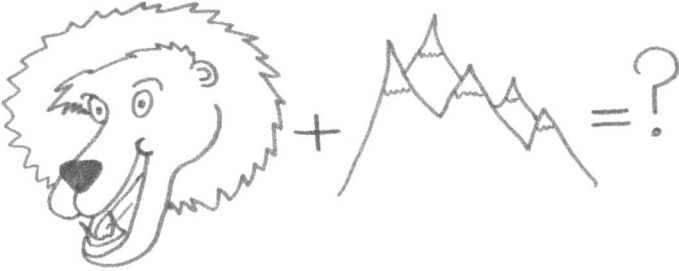

Breakfast:

Hmm, I'm having a browse through the boxes of cereals in the cupboard, bypassing the Tupperware container of muesli and reaching for some chocolate flavour puffed rice cereals and making a cup of tea. My son is already happily munching away on a bowl of the cereals. Fair play to him, he gets himself up and sorts out his own breakfast from time to time. Not bad for an eight year old. I'm now sitting with him, crunching away watching Spongebob Squarepants.

I've got a bit of time before work so I shall make something to take for lunch. A quick look in the fridge shows that there is still a big wedge of lamb left so I shall carve off some slices and make lamb sandwiches. I'm a bit worried that if I put mint sauce on them and eat it later, I may have a forest of green minty bits all over my teeth and frighten the customers. I wonder if mustard would go.....I don't see why not. Lashings of it, yum, looking forward to this.

Pop one of these so called "fun size" bananas and a chocolate biscuit into a carrier bag along with the sandwiches and I'm all set to go.

Mid morning:

Having a cup of tea to warm up as it's a bit parky today. As I typed that, the spell checker went berserk. Parky might be a colloquialism then, but here in the West country it means a bit chilly, and it certainly is that today. The last few nights in fact have been colder than usual and so our wood burner has been working overtime. It's surprising how much wood you can go through if you don't "pace" it. Since getting the wood burner I've turned into a scavenger, I even found myself going through a bin outside a DIY store as I could see some wood sticking out of the top. I was amazed to see what was being thrown away and it gave me a few hours of free heat.

Nibbling on the chocolate biscuit and having a sneaky dunk while no customers are looking. Delicious.

Not massively hungry at the moment so I will try and have lunch later today as it makes the dreary pointless afternoon seem to go quicker.

People are weird aren't they? When you work in a shop, you have to balance your enthusiasm with some level of etiquette. You know what it's like when you go into a large electrical store just to have a look at something. Within seconds of the doors swooshing closed behind you as you enter the store, a gaggle of sales people are falling over themselves to get to you and thrusting their opinions and special offers on you.

In this shop, as a small local business, we tend not to pounce on people as they come in, but give them a while just to browse and then drop in a gentle "are you OK there? Do you need any help?". What confuses me is when people say "No, I'm fine thanks, I don't need any help, do you sell......?" and then ask for something even though they don't need help!!

Either you need help or you don't. See? I told you this would have a few rants in it.

Lunchtime:

I fancy a cup of coffee but it has a terrible habit of rendering my bowels incapable of hanging on to their contents, maybe that's something else that comes with age, so I will go for a cup of tea instead and enjoy the curious flavour that it has after eating one of the mustard soaked lamb sandwiches.

It's been a strange old morning again with people ringing up the shop and asking questions mainly about animals. That never ceases to amaze me, I mean, if you had a dog that was ill or a hamster that needed medical attention, wouldn't you take it to a vet? Perhaps people are looking for a cheaper answer.

A lady came in today and said that her dog was starting to "stiffen up" and she wondered if collagen tablets might be helpful. I asked her if it was a Pointer. She didn't see the funny side. Anyway, I've seen enough people suffering with arthritis start to take collagen tablets, have really good results and come back for more. Strangely enough, we even have a lady who comes in and buys lots and lots of it for her horses, so I had no hesitation in suggesting these.

To decide whether a high or low dose tablet would be suitable, I asked how big the dog was and she said it weighed 13 stone. I know a few humans that weigh less than that, so the high dose seemed appropriate. Curiosity got the better of me and I asked what sort of dog it was. The lady quite proudly told me it was a Leonberger and then gave me some additional information regarding the background of this breed.

According to the owner, Leon means Lion. So far, so good, I can see the logic in that. Next the lady tells me that Berger means mountain in German. My limited knowledge of German confirms that to be almost fairly accurate. Then she goes on to tell me that they are called this because they were used centuries ago to hunt mountain lions in the German Alps. Hmm, I don't have the heart to tell her that they come from a German town called Leonberg, west of Stuttgart and the nearest they've ever come to a lion is probably watching one on the Discovery Channel. I won't burst her bubble, not today anyway.

Teatime:

A rather splendid smell of curry greets me as I walk in through the front door, so I'm guessing that's what we are having for tea.
Chicken Jalfrezi with rice and a garlic and coriander naan bread, washed down with a can of diet coke. Yes, that's the diet part. This is all served up in bowls rather than on a plate to reduce the portion size. I tend to find that the rice fills me up and so I'm guessing/hoping that I won't snack through the evening.

Day 8- Your Food Diary

Breakfast

Mid Morning

Lunchtime

Teatime

Other snacks

Day 9 Tuesday - A Social Scientist?

Breakfast:

I've gone with an easy option of corn flakes this morning and a cup of tea. I think I slept fairly well last night, but you can never be sure. I know I dreamt of some weird things like trying to wee in a crowded place and not being able to go because everyone wanted to watch. Go on then, all you amateur psychiatrists, tell me what it means. Some deep rooted fear of water, stemming from when I drowned as a child? Yeah, right!

Mid morning:

Dad's just been on the phone with one of his suppliers (makes him sound like a drug lord or something) and she has confirmed a few things that he already knew but had hoped were untrue.

My knowledge of this is somewhat sketchy at the moment but the gist of it is this: Back in 2004 some legislation was passed that stated in effect that some, if not all, herbal medicines were to be banned from sale to the public from April 2011.

If you believe some of the details on the internet, this action has been thoroughly encouraged by large pharmaceutical companies who are insisting that their mind altering, organ destroying drugs are to be more accessible than thousands of years worth of knowledge and natural relief. As an example, milk thistle is something that is used to help liver function. A relative of mine uses it to try and repair some of the damage that he has inflicted on himself over the years, however, in April 2011 it will no longer be able to be displayed, let alone sold to members of the public. There are some concessions that state all existing stock can be sold until they run out, but after that....that's it.

The list of things that are being banned is growing, but so far it seems that a large percentage of the shop's stock may soon become contraband, just to pick a random fraction from the air, I would hazard a guess at maybe 50% of the stock having to be removed and therefore half of my parents income, which in turn could have a knock on effect on my income. Time will tell and I will do an update at the end of the thirty days.

I don't want to get into politics but although we all know how corrupt it is and always has been, recent events including the bale out of the banks, and crazy laws being passed that only benefit the super rich companies, really highlights the poor state of the world in general and how bizarrely they throw money at pointless, barely legal, time consuming activities, which leads me on to my next rant and it's not even 11am.

A customer came in just now, I say just now, it was more like an hour ago. Dad recognised her from a previous visit and happened to remark "you're a scientist aren't you?, Been doing any experiments lately?". He wasn't actually interested, it was just general shopkeeper chat to fill the gap between the customer paying and receiving their change. However the customer took it as an invitation to launch into nearly an hour long explanation of what she does and of what great importance it is to the well-being, smooth running and long term prosperity of the nation.

Basically, I think deep down, she was trying to justify to herself the probably extortionate salary she is paid for what in my opinion is a fruitless and pointless waste of time. She may as well be making chocolate teapots.

The short version of this is that she and a colleague (so that's double the extortionate salary) carry out "studies" that assess the effect of things such as the flooding that took place in various parts of the UK. So in essence, they go to the place that has just been flooded or bombed or anthraxed, clutching a clip board, no doubt wearing a fluorescent high visibility jacket and ask the victims such dumb ass questions as "so, are you happy that your belongings are now a pile of sludge?", "In what way would you say that this experience has enriched your life?"

At the end of this heartless study, the gleaners of such worthless and obvious answers return to the comfort of their plush hotels (possibly and hopefully nursing at least one black eye each) to type up the results onto their impossibly expensive laptops. Weeks later when the oh-so important result is finally agreed on and printed up as a leather bound volume, it turns out that the study found….and excuse me for using more than the usual socially acceptable number of exclamation marks….the study found that the victims of the flood were less than happy about it!!!!!!!!!!!!!!!!!!!!!!!!!!!!!!!!

As if that wasn't bad enough, I am writing this during a particularly long stretch of bad weather, and whilst I could rant about how pathetic this country is at dealing with a whole inch of snow, I will confine myself to letting you know what their current study is on. Yes, you've guessed it, its about how the bad weather has affected people and how they feel about it, for example, does it make them feel happy or sad!

I could cry, I'm so exasperated by this woman and the sheer waste of money that is poured into this type of stuff. And to top it off, she had a really loud, irritating voice. My head is pounding. These Social Scientists probably used to work for the department that came up with the "five a day" rule.

Lunchtime:

Lunchtime's here and I'm so cross that I can't be bothered with healthy eating, so it's a bag of chips, a battered sausage and some curry sauce. And if there's a survey somewhere, some social scientist wondering how I'm feeling about my lunch and wishing to produce a report on it, I'm very, very pleased about it and I shall enjoy eating it and probably have great joy later forcing it from my ample butt, so stick that in your report!!!!!!!!!!!!!!!!!!!!!!!!

Ooh I'm livid. I need to calm down a bit. There's not many things that set me off, but that was one of them. I could find myself running out of exclamation marks at this rate. Have some more!!!!!!

Teatime:

Had a crappy afternoon. Not particularly good use of the English language but there's no other word for it. I think that woman wound me up so much that everything else was tainted by that. What a shame.

Right then. Ah, I forgot to tell my wife that I went and bought chips for lunch and so she has done chips for tea with some fish. My first thought is to wonder how many bones will be in the fish. You know how they put a flue pipe down chimneys to help fumes escape safely? I wonder if they could do the same for the human throat and protect it from fish bones on the way down.

As it happens, I only found three bones in this fish, so that's not bad (for me). I've got a chocolate pudding for dessert but I think I will save it for later as I'm pretty full from this and my angry lunch.

Supper time:

Tucking into a microwaved chocolate pudding, you know the sort. You think "oh, the outside isn't that warm" and then your spoon melts as it reaches the molten lava inside the pudding and your eyeballs shrivel from the heat of the nuked chocolate sauce. Very tasty though and washed down with a large glass of sweet white wine, only something cheap like a Liebfraumilch, but it's doing the trick. I wonder if I will dream weird things tonight. I'm not too concerned though as I have the day off tomorrow.

Day 9- Your Food Diary

Breakfast

Mid Morning

Lunchtime

Teatime

Other snacks

Day 10 Wednesday - "My God, ziss tastes like bleach!"

Breakfast:

Fear and trepidation awaken within me and a feeling of anxiety trickles down my neck, because today, my son's school has put out the invitation for parents and carers to join their offspring for school dinners. So, I need to choose a breakfast that will fill me up so that I'm not too hungry at lunchtime.

I've gone for some wheat based cereals that seem to be doing the trick of filling me up and a cup of tea.

Lunchtime:

Here we go, at the school now and queuing with one very excited son. Hmm, I'm not sure I like the way the dinner lady is glaring at me and gripping her spoon. We're getting nearer the serving hatch now and I'm reminded of TV shows based in prisons where they slop the food into a plastic tray. Oh, look, a pile of plastic trays with little compartments for the various coloured slops. Crikey, they could do with a clean, they're filthy.

As I get nearer, I can see there is a choice of what the lady is calling chicken pie and something she is referring to as fish fingers, although they look like they have been injured in some bizarre farmyard battle, so with this bewildering array of choice I copy what my more experienced son has done and go for the so called "chicken pie". We're now shuffling along to the pudding hatch where the dangerous lady is still glaring at me and hitting the palm of her hand with the spoon.

Once again there is a choice, sponge cake, and here's the choice part, with lemon sauce or without lemon sauce. Now my son has gone for the sauce-less option but I think I'm being a bit wise here and going for the moist choice, and yet as she slops what looks like used dishwater onto the cake without ever breaking eye contact with me, I'm already starting to think I should have skipped the sauce.

I'm heading for the cutlery now and trying to find a knife and fork not stuck together with yesterdays lunches. There's definitely a knack to this and I don't have it. I generally had a packed lunch in school all those years ago or went to my Nan's where she would spoil me rotten.

Trying to find a comfortable way to sit on the tiny school chairs without my knees tipping the table and without the entire miniature chair inserting itself any further up my sphincter. I've ended up in a position which is half doing the jazz splits and halfway to using one of those nasty French "hole in the ground" toilets.

I'm looking around now to see if they have a mallet so I can get my knife through what they have passed off as chicken pie. A quick glance around the table shows me that the kids have already got this worked out and have turned the chicken pie over and are starting from the underneath where a small amount of moisture appears to be held around the solitary sweet corn within. From this point, they work outwards and then leave the armour coated crust to one side before they start on the rubber potato wedges which put me in mind of the shredded tyres you see along the side of a motorway.

After enduring that, I'm already feeling guilty about subjecting my child to this farce on a weekly basis. I reach for a plastic cup of water and cut my lip on the edge of the rim which has been chewed by generations of school kids, maybe in an attempt to fill their bellies with something slightly softer than the chicken pie.

The sponge cake appears from time to time in the "pudding compartment" of the plastic tray, bobbing around in the so called lemon sauce. Opposite me is one of my son's friends, he has Romanian relatives and a slight accent. He has attempted to have some of the sauce-drenched sponge and with a look on his face like he's licked a nettle exclaims "My God, ziss tastes like bleach". Never has an eight year old been more accurate.

So all in all, I would say, if you ever have the opportunity to sample a school dinner, go for it. It will open your eyes and may encourage you to give your child a packed lunch. Even if things are financially hard, whatever you provide, a simple packed lunch containing a ham sandwich, an apple, cheese, eggs, anything has to be better than this pile of nastiness. My heart and my colon goes out to all the kids who ate this stuff.

I have a burning sensation in my chest where the lemon sauce is eating away at all my internal organs and stripping them of bacteria, both good and bad. I need to go home and have something to take away the taste but I'm hiccuping now and keep re-living the sauce episode over and over again. I'd like to say it's a value for money moment, but it certainly isn't.

Teatime:

A number of hours have passed since the lunchtime episode, four and a half to be precise and I'm hoping that my tea tonight will be a powerfully flavoured dish that might get rid of the evil lemon taste in my mouth and throat and stomach.

Thankfully my wife has served up chilli con carne, heavy on the chilli, light on the carne. Some garlic bread and a pint of shandy all help to wipe out the memory of my lunch. I look across the table at my son and simply say "I'm sorry buddy". He just smiles. He knows exactly what I mean.

Day 10- Your Food Diary

Breakfast

Mid Morning

Lunchtime

Teatime

Other snacks

Day 11 - Thursday - Thank you Jeffrey Archer

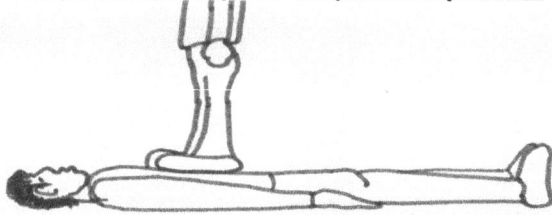

Breakfast:

I'm getting a bit bored with cereals, so I pondered over a loaf of bread this morning debating whether to have toast or not, but then noticed there was an awful lot of mould on the edges and it put me off. Having peered into the back of the cupboard, a perilous endeavour at the best of times, I have come across a box containing sachets of oats. It says on here just to add some milk and microwave the contents for a hearty breakfast. I have to say I'm not mightily convinced, I mean for a start, the sachet is only about 4 inches square. Unless the milk re-hydrates a full English breakfast hidden somewhere within the packet, I wouldn't say it falls into the category of a hearty breakfast.

Nevertheless, lets give it a go.

As I suspected , this is more of a heartless breakfast than a hearty one. I'm fairly sure I will need to refuel before lunchtime. I will try and think healthy thoughts and keep busy though and try and rinse these oats from the roof of my mouth with a cup of tea.

Mid-morning:

I feel like I'm wasting away and about to black out, I've also got the shakes a bit. I have thought that maybe I'm heading towards diabetes but all tests so far have shown otherwise. Perhaps I'm just greedy. I think I shall buy a yoghurt topped apricot flapjack just to keep me going. Previous experience has told me not to look at the calories in it though. Oh, go on, just a quick peek, and the peek turns to an eek. Yet again a billion butter soaked calories heading for my stomach. At least the shakes have gone, although I'm not sure if that's because I've eaten or if it's simply a matter of physics and something as large as my body can't possibly generate enough motion to shake for a very long time. Where's a scientist when you need them to answer a question, but then, having heard some of the things they've said in recent years, I think I may be better off not knowing.

Lunchtime:

At last, it's lunchtime and I peel open a foil wrapped packet that contains sandwiches made from the rather suspect bread I saw (and rejected) this morning. Contained within these mouldy slices, my wife has combined, to my delight, jam and cheese. Yes, I know some people are gagging at the thought, but it's a combination that works so well for my palette. Perhaps it shows a less than prestigious upbringing, but what the heck. I shall even ignore the mould and tuck straight in.

A swift and sizeable chomp tells me that I needn't have worried about the mould. My ever fastidious wife has sprayed the wooden chopping board that she made the sandwiches on, with a lemon scented anti bacterial spray. This has not only added an extra lemony dimension of flavour to the bread, but also kills off any nasties that may be lurking in the mould. I am suddenly put in mind of school dinners. How strange.

I'm working with my mother this afternoon and she is a little concerned with my health at the moment as I am bent double with chest pains and my left arm and the left side of my face are tingling and a little bit numb. You may be thinking it's the mouldy bread or anti-bacterial spray or perhaps I'm having a heart attack, but I've had these pains on and off for years. Even in school as a 7 or 8 year old I remember asking a boy called Jeffrey Archer (obviously not THE Jeffrey Archer) to stand on my chest as I lay on the floor. This was the only way to relieve the pains I felt, also there was a two-fold positive result to this. First, I felt relief and second, he found great amusement in doing that for me. I'm not sure I ever thanked him, so thank you Jeffrey Archer wherever you are, but you could have wiped your feet first.

My Mum thinks it's a trapped nerve that's causing my pain, it's a theory that has been put to me before and here's a weird thing. Mum just told me to touch my toes to stretch the muscles in my back, so I did, and then she sort of wedged her knuckles into some crevice on my back and the pain over my chest was excruciating. When she stopped, the pain stopped, so it does seem to be a nerve related problem, she even gave the nerve a name, not like Bob or Simon, but the medical name for it. Apparently it runs from the back, around the side and over the chest. Damn painful what ever it's called.

Teatime:

Lasagne and garlic bread for tea. This could be good, as long as the anti bacterial spray has been out of reach during the preparation of this. Occasionally my wife makes a passable attempt at lasagne, it's a promising sign that I've even recognised what it's meant to be.

The best lasagne I ever had was in a little tea shop in a village called Dunster, in Somerset way back in 1988. A group of about 30 of us decided for some reason that it would be good fun to play 'cops and robbers' in the woods surrounding the castle at Dunster and split into two groups. So we muddied up our faces commando style and hid in piles of leaves and up trees. Whoever was caught by the 'cops' became a cop and so on until we were all caught. By the time we had finished we were all filthy and dishevelled and entirely ravenous so we headed to the shops and pubs in the village at the bottom of the hill, below the castle. If you've ever been there, you will have seen the yarn market, a circular building that dates back from 1590 (as shown in the photo along with my son's foot) and is listed as an ancient monument and will be for some time yet unless the ever increasing flow of lorries through the narrow village keep clipping bits off the edge of it.

Anyway, as it was now lunch time, the majority of the pubs had all filled up with tourists so we trekked along the cobbles until we came to a teashop that had lots of tables still empty and piled in, looking very much like a group of extras from a Robin Hood film. The staff were a little taken aback but nevertheless welcomed us and took our orders. I think most of us ordered the lasagne and so it took a while to arrive. But when it did, oh boy, melt in the mouth pasta, layers of creamy fluffy white sauce in between layers of tasty beefy minced meat with onions and herbs, topped with a gently bronzed parmesan crust. Home made

chunky chips on the side and a pint of cold shandy (I was driving) ,I
thought I had died and gone to heaven.

Unfortunately that place was taken over by new management some
time after and the lasagne was never the same, but the memories linger,
as does my wife's lasagne.

Day 11- Your Food Diary

Breakfast

Mid Morning

Lunchtime

Teatime

Other snacks

Day 12 - Friday – An Electrode Each.

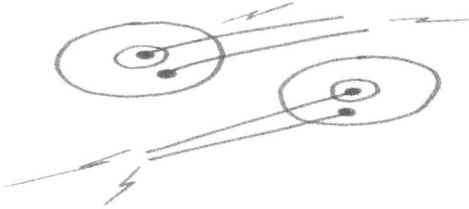

Breakfast:

I'm rushing a bit as I slept very deeply and have to take my son to school today. At the moment I have most Fridays off and use it to catch up on jobs that need doing, like chopping wood, or scavenging for more wood, or paperwork that builds up.

I don't feel too good today, a bit giddy and can't be bothered to make something fancy for breakfast, so I'm just going for chocolate cookie cereals and a cup of tea. I've got a plan I want to try next week involving having protein for breakfast. No point trying it until then as the weekends are sort of unstructured as far as eating and mealtimes go.

Mid morning:

I came back from the school and was out of breath and now have a thumping headache. I shall see how that goes. I tend to try and avoid taking tablets if I can, but this is banging.

I just tried to carry some sacks of wood through to the back garden to put in the wood store I built. They're not particularly heavy but I've gone dizzy and dropped to my knees, my left arm and hand are tingling again and my heart is beating so hard it feels like the bridge of my nose and top of my head are going to explode. I have to say that at this point it would be easy to panic a bit, but I'm trying to stay calm. I notice that my skin is not clammy or damp in any way and in the back of my mind I seem to recall that's a good thing. If I fall down flat, I shall try and aim to be near the telephone.

69

A few minutes have passed and things seem to have settled down, so I try and get up from my knees and head to the kitchen for a glass of water as I feel really thirsty. Wow, such a simple thing took great effort and once again it's all started, my heart nearly thumping out of my chest, I can't breathe very well and I'm so dizzy that I'm clutching at the walls and door frame like a drunk. It's a miracle that I can type this with my big clammy hands(ha ha, I'm typing this later in the day).

Because of the similarities between yesterdays chest pains and this, I'm not convinced that it is a trapped nerve. Could that really cause me such discomfort and make my heart race like this? I know trapped nerves can be uncomfortable as I've suffered with sciatica for years, not constantly, but just now and then it will catch, my knees will buckle and a shooting pain will go like a needle through my bum cheek and down my leg. But this is different.

The chest pains, like I mentioned before, have been there since I was a kid, and even in recent years it happened again. The pain got so bad and the numbness in my left arm made me think I was having a heart attack, so I drove myself to the hospital. Not the best idea I suppose but it was only half a mile away so I felt I could manage that. I sat in the accident and emergency waiting room for a bit and fair enough to them, they pushed me to the head of the queue as the symptoms were quite severe and I was clutching my chest.

After wiring me up to some beeping machine and gluing the little wire bits to my hairy chest, they left me to beep away for nearly a whole hour. Then the nurse came back and tore off what looked like a very long till receipt and said that she would give this to a doctor to look at and that he would return and tell me what the hell was going on. About two hours later, a doctor came up to me and informed me that I hadn't had a heart attack, there was nothing wrong with me and that I have the heart of a buffalo. The pains were most likely caused by muscle spasms. I questioned him for a while as this didn't really feel like a good explanation for the pains I had felt, and I knew for sure that I hadn't imagined them. He however said he was busy and that this was a perfectly good explanation for what I had experienced, so I should shut up and go home now.

I have to say I wasn't particularly pleased with the verdict or his attitude but the pains had stopped and I don't like being in hospitals, so I did pack up and go home. Just before that, the nurse ripped off two of the four electrode pads that were stuck into the hair on my chest, chuckled to herself and muttered something about having her bikini line waxed. I had heard while I was in hospital that my sister in law and my foody friend were at my house waiting to see if I was OK, so I asked the nurse to leave two electrodes on for them to rip off. They're both odd like that and I do my little bit to amuse them from time to time. So when I got home, I offered them an electrode each and they happily tugged away, rather too slowly, removing chest hairs one by painful one.

Lunchtime:

Not feeling too hungry at the moment but at least the pain has subsided and seems to have settled down. Think I will just have a tin of tomatoes with some bread. It fills you up and should see me through until teatime and it's so easy to make. My wife thinks it's disgusting but it's something that is from my childhood and I remember having it for lunch on Saturday's in a plastic bowl sitting in my go-kart, which had a sort of box section that could keep the wind and rain off of me if I angled it right.

In the back was a secret compartment in which I always had a bag of toffee bonbons and a few of those small Beano or Dandy comics that cost 20p. In time I fitted a light in there and a curtain across the front. If you can picture in your mind a changing room in a department store, the sort with curtains, not doors. Now in this picture, put wheels on the bottom. That's pretty much what my go kart looked like.

I remember one dark winters evening my cousin Lisa coming around for tea with her parents and I set her and my little sister up in there with a blanket, hot water bottle, some sweets and the light, which I think had a 10 meter lead on it and plugged into the cigarette lighter of my dads blue Fiat 123. They sat there for hours and Lisa read stories to my sister. They seemed to enjoy the novelty of it and our parents had a few hours peace and a flat car battery the next day.

Anyway, back to the tomato bread. Tip some of the juice into the bottom of the pan, pop a slice or two of bread in there and empty the rest of the tin of tomatoes on top. Heat, stir and mush it up. A sprinkling of salt, tip it in a bowl and away we go. A strangely satisfying "meal".

Teatime:

I wasn't sure that I would feel like eating after the chest pains, but as the day has worn on and the pains have subsided, I'm starting to feel a bit peckish. My wife is feeling a bit grim tonight so I think I will make something for tea. I will make what I call a risotto, but technically, it probably isn't because I'm not using risotto rice, just short grain brown bog standard rice.

I shall cook the onions first and then add all the bits and pieces including chicken stock. I'm sure I read somewhere that you should add the stock a bit at a time, but to be honest, I cant be bothered today, so it's all getting bunged in a saucepan and put on a low heat while I go and sit down.

Gordon Ramsey would be ashamed of me.

Well, I have to say, that didn't taste too bad at all. We all cleared our bowls, even my son. My daughter and me fought over the remains and split the "seconds" between us. A good result for a simple dish and we're all full now.

Day 12- Your Food Diary

Breakfast

Mid Morning

Lunchtime

Teatime

Other snacks

73

Day 13 - Saturday - Funny shaped head.

Breakfast:

I woke in the night with a cunning plan. Funny how these thoughts come to you at the strangest times. I was thinking of the silly little sachet of oats I had a day or two ago and thought…wait for it….ground breaking stuff this. Why not have two! In the same bowl!

Mind you, having done the two sachets now it's not filling me with glee, it's not filling me with anything at all. If you laid out the contents of these two packets on a tray it might cover 6 square inches to a depth of 4mm. I think a sparrow could throw up more than this after a night on the town. My cup of tea might help to fill my empty stomach.

Obviously the idea of having oats for breakfast is nothing new. The good old Scots still swear by it and avoid any of the fancy sugared up brands with added fruity bits. Apparently, and I've not yet tried this, a pinch of salt goes well in your porridge. I think I will stick with maple syrup. I know it's quite sugary but I do find oats a little bland without something added. My Great Grandfather who was from Glasgow would turn in his grave.

Lunchtime:

We went out with some friends this morning, it was quite cold so I'm feeling like I need a warm lunch rather than just a sandwich. I've just found a packet of couscous in the cupboard, that's a quick and easy lunch, pour it into a bowl, boil the kettle and tip it over the couscous and wait five minutes. As it's a tasteless sort of grain I'm going to put a powdered chicken soup mix in with it so that it absorbs the flavour.

I'm tempted to add a knob of butter but I think I shall resist the temptation and hope that my reward at the end of the 30 days will be obvious. The chest pains have made me a bit more focussed on thinking about what I eat and how much of it I shovel into my body. Whether or not this will translate into action, is very much down to me and how I feel on a daily basis.

Well, that's lunch sorted and even the kids had a bowl of it and didn't complain, so that's got to be good.

Teatime:

I've got a banging headache again. I went through a period of about 4 years with almost constant headaches. The doctors always said it was high blood pressure but my Mum suggested that I went to an osteopath and get them to check out my spine and neck and head. I have to say I was a bit sceptical but decided to give it a go. When I got to the osteopath's I filled in some forms and then was shown upstairs to a light and airy room with high ceilings and a large window looking out over some trees at the back of the building. In the middle of the room was one of those beds they use for massage, the one with the hole in it for your face. My son saw one of these tables at my parents shop once as they used to have a therapy centre above it. As usual he looked at it for a while, pondered and then said "dad, is that where your balls go?"

I suppose they could, but today I'm rather assuming that my face was going to be in there.

A small, petite, attractive blonde lady gets up from the chair in the corner by a very neatly stocked desk, shakes my hand and asks me to take my top off and sit on the bed, which she expertly covers with one movement of her left hand, unrolling what looks like a massive toilet roll. It's the sort of size I could imagine me needing if I continue to get fatter. Anyway, shuffling up onto the bed I cant help but wonder what on earth this tiny woman, whose handshake I barely felt, can do for a great big bloke like me.

She asks some questions about what I do for a living, how much exercise I do, how old I am and then asks me to lean forward. She presses her hands into my back and it feels like she is harvesting my organs as they move around and around. Next she performs a move that took me a little by surprise and I'm not even sure it's politically correct but she asks me to lie down on my back again and then sort of climbs up on me. She places my right hand on my left shoulder and my left hand on my right shoulder, so I'm laying there like an Egyptian mummy. Then she pulls me up toward her and has me in a surprisingly tight 'hug'.

"I'm going to count to three and I need you to breathe out and then I'm going to turn you slightly" she says softly in my ear.

"will it hurt?" I ask.

"No, not at all" she says. "OK, one, two, three"

Next, a surprisingly powerful movement for such a small woman and a cracking noise that comes from deep within me and yet is so loud that it drowns out the pained, shocked noise that comes out of my mouth.

" I thought you said it wouldn't hurt" I said looking at her like a smacked child.

"I lied" she said quite matter of factly and climbed off of me.

Apparently the headaches I had been suffering for four years or more, were being caused by me having two ribs out of place. The only time I can think I may have done this is when I fell on my back snowboarding about four years ago. So the dates coincide. Otherwise, I have no explanation as to how two of my ribs decided to move out of their usual residence. Perhaps they were being ribbed by the other bones. Do you see what I did there? Rib, ribbed. See?

I went back again a few weeks later for a follow up treatment half hoping that she might try at least the first part of that move on me again, but instead she did cranial osteopathy on me. Now I'd never heard of this before but she explained that your skull is made up of different

76

plates of bone that can move about. When I said I'd never heard about this before, I knew that when babies are born the bones in their head are mobile and over time fuse together, but I didn't know that as adults it could still happen.

So, I'm laying on the bed thing face up and the tiny woman, whose name escapes me, is sat behind me holding my head in her small but dangerous hands and starts mashing my head like it's some sort of stress toy.

"Hmm", she says, "you've got a funny shaped head"

"Oh thanks very much" I replied thinking that she was being a bit over familiar with me, but then I remembered that she had climbed on top of me when I wasn't wearing a shirt a few weeks previous. In some countries that would probably mean we were married by now.

"and you had quite a difficult birth didn't you?" she continued.

Like I said before, I've been sceptical in the past about these sort of treatments, but there's no way she could have known about my birth as I'm fairly certain she wasn't there, but I did indeed have a bad time at my birth. My mother went into labour and, missing out all the messy details, I was pulled out by the head with a massive pair of salad tongs three days later, so maybe I have got a funny shaped head and possibly some lettuce and tomato embedded in there somewhere.

The conversation stopped there and I just lay quietly as she continued to manipulate my skull and jiggle my brain. Suddenly I felt an overwhelming urge to giggle but resisted it as long as I possibly could without wetting myself and then I could hold it no longer and chuckled out loud.

I apologised and explained the emotion I had experienced out of nowhere. She said it was perfectly normal and I may experience other emotions too, so I settled down and she started again. About 5 minutes passed and the sun must have gone behind a cloud or something as the room darkened and I felt an unbearable pool of sadness well up inside of me and I started to sob like a baby. It occurred to me later that maybe I was just upset because she had said I had a funny shaped head.

Thirty minutes passed and I went from giggling to crying to nearly dropping off to sleep to feeling very invigorated and could also breathe properly through my nostrils, which doesn't happen very often due to sinus trouble.

Apart from the trauma of being wrenched emotionally and physically in knots, my experience of osteopathy was certainly interesting and the persistent headaches I had experienced for so long disappeared. I am a sceptic no more.

However, today's headache is still there so I will take a few tablets with my food, which is unusual for me. I don't know why, I don't have a particular aversion to tablets but I do try and let things run their natural course, even headaches, but today this is getting me down. It feels like someone has put a tumble drier in my forehead and it's constantly throbbing.

Strangely enough it's putting me off of my food a little, I just need to lie down. So I will quietly work my way through the sausages, mash, peas and gravy on my plate and "shush" at the kids now and then before my head explodes.

Off to bed now. Need to get more sleep. Beauty sleep in particular and let these tablets do their job.

Day 13- Your Food Diary

Breakfast

Mid Morning

Lunchtime

Teatime

Other snacks

Day 14 - Sunday - 1000 sit-ups and Big Paul

Breakfast:

I've decided to start the day with some muesli. I haven't been a great fan of muesli as some years ago I broke a tooth on some hard object hidden away amongst the oats and nuts. I'm still not exactly sure what it was that was in there, but when I spat out bits of tooth, there seemed to be a stone or something similar mingled in. I mean like a stone from the road as opposed to a stone from a cherry or something. So with a little caution I shall munch through this bowlful of nuts and fruit, trying not to bite down too hard.

I've got the urge to have a cup of coffee but I know I will make it and then regret it or suffer the dire consequences later as the wrath of the caffeine goes to war against my bowel. A cup of tea will be a safer bet.

Lunchtime:

I've managed to avoid snacking through the morning so I am feeling a bit peckish. I can smell meat of some sort roasting in the kitchen but I'm not sure yet what it is. I shall go and sneak a peek. Although I don't know why I'm sneaking, I live here too.

OK, it's one of those supermarket joints of meat in a foil tray. According to the box it used to be a chicken although it's completely unrecognisable as such as it sits bubbling away in my oven. If chickens believe in Hell, this must be it. I'm always concerned that after 2 hours in my oven, something like this can still look like it's never seen the light of day.

I'm being chased from the kitchen now by my wife brandishing an electric carving knife. I'm amazed that thing still works, the knife, not my wife, it was a wedding present 21 years ago, but has been useful and carved a range of things from crusty bread right through to beautiful joints of beef and on one occasion, shoe leather.

When we lived in Wales, a meat van would drive around the little towns and villages. When I say meat van, I don't mean a van made of meat. That would just be impractical and raise a whole host of health and safety issues. The vehicle looked like a furniture removal van with a big side flap that opened up, turning it into a counter from which the men concealed within could sell meat. It always shocked me that so many people could be hidden away inside the freezer section of such a van without dying.

When it would turn up at Llantrisant Market at 6am and put up lists of what was for sale that particular day it was always about half the price of the supermarket meat and for £10 you could get a huge joint of beef that would feed ten or more people, or you could cut it up into smaller joints and freeze them. For £5 you could get ten or so chicken breasts or choose from a dazzling array of sausages. I know a few people questioned the hygiene of this system and refused to buy from it, but we did for many years and never had even a sniff of food poisoning.

Anyway, no such joints of joy today, just this anaemic ball of meat bubbling in it's own tears.

I do love roast potatoes. They can make or break a meal I think. If you've ever had a roast dinner without roasties you will know what I mean. There's something missing, it doesn't matter how many extra types of vegetables someone may cram onto the plate. If there aren't roasties, it's not complete. Thankfully today I have them steaming away in all their carbohydrated glory sitting proudly next to some gleaming sprouts that are waiting to release their gasses into me. Carrots and roast parsnips complete the picture and are smothered in thick hot gravy.

The slices of roast anaemia are actually not too bad, and of course, lashings of mint sauce help to make the whole lunchtime experience a pleasant one. Wash it all down with some excessively sweet supermarket sparkling "wine" and I think we all need an afternoon kip.

Teatime:

Phew, still quite full from my lunch and actually a bit bloated, in fact my stomach is poking out over the top of my trousers and looking like the bonnet of a strangely shaped car (that's "hood" in the U.S.). I certainly wouldn't win any prizes for aerodynamics here.

As we are all full from lunch we are just having some cheese and ham rolls with some crisps and a cup of tea. I've been sat here like an old man, hugging my mug of tea staring into the flames of the wood burner.

It's not nice getting older is it? I mean in some ways it is because you get more freedom and choice in what you're doing and you don't have homework or school problems to contend with, but when you walk past the mirror and see what gravity, weather, sleepless nights, worry and a whole host of other adult issues are doing to the way you look, it can be sad.

I'm looking in the mirror now and thinking back 20 or so years to when I lived in Cardiff in a damp flat in a street called New Zealand Road, just off of North Road, one of the main roads going into the centre of Cardiff. I had a friend called Paul Evans, a lovely bloke, about 6'4", unassuming and quietly spoken with a thick Cardiff accent. We called him Big Paul. I think his Mum was Greek as he had that healthy, swarthy look about him that made women turn their heads as he walked by.

Anyway, we had decided that we wanted to do some exercise on a regular basis and made arrangements to go to the gym at least once or twice a week to do some weight training. Big Paul wanted to bulk up a bit so that his frame matched his height. I just needed to do some form of exercise and have someone there to encourage me as I'm not very good at motivating myself to go to the gym alone. We did this for a while and had some fairly good results.

The process of me working on my arms, shoulders and chest had the effect of giving me that "V" shape all the health magazines refer to, so I was pleased and also my stomach was as flat as road kill. But there was no visible 6 pack. I knew one was in there, but it just wouldn't show itself, so I thought that sit-ups would do the trick. Every morning before work I would wake up and do 500 sit-ups and when I came home from work I would do 500 more. My goodness, you would think that I looked like a rapper on an album cover wouldn't you, but no. Not a thing showing through. The one thing I did get though was haemorrhoids, great big juicy ones ironically in the shape of a six pack, but not in a place where anyone could see them.

Over-eating and office life then took it's toll on me as I mentioned at the beginning and I started to assume the shape I am now. I did read years later that, if you want to have your six pack showing, you need to have less than 6 percent body fat, or was it 12 percent? I cant remember but I know it was something that I never achieved and now probably never will. Maybe I should get concave mirrors.

I wonder what happened to Big Paul, we lost touch when I moved from Cardiff. The last thing I heard was that he was working as a carpenter and living in the Llandaff area. So, if you see a 6'4" Greek looking man called Paul sawing a piece of wood, tell him I said "Hi".

Right, now it's time to see the news and try and have an early night. Often there's not much point in going to bed early as my wife has panic attacks and wakes me up anyway, but that's a story for another time. Good night cruel world.

Day 14- Your Food Diary

Breakfast

Mid Morning

Lunchtime

Teatime

Other snacks

Day 15 - Monday - Special Panty Pads.

Breakfast:

Now you may remember that a few days ago, or to be precise, a few nights ago, I awoke from a deep sleep, dazzling myself with a cunning plan. This was the oat eating plan but I also had the thought that if I ate protein for breakfast, it may fill me up for longer. So today I am going to start my day with some scrambled egg and a cup of tea. I probably could do without the cup of tea but it's sort of a habit or maybe even a tradition now.

Two eggs and a splash of milk in a pint jug, whisk it up and season it with salt and pepper and bang it in the microwave. Actually I didn't bang it in, I placed it very gently in there, I'm quite a gentle man for my size, but don't think I couldn't kill you with one hand if you cross me. Ooh scary, don't know where that came from. I guess it's that dreaded "Monday feeling" surfacing and I'm tired and hungry, a usually bad combination.

I think three or four minutes should do this. PING, the microwave calls to me and a quick check tells me that it's ready. Microwave scrambled egg is always more pale and more fluffy than if you do it in a saucepan. I don't know why, maybe it cooks differently, don't microwaves cook things from the inside out? Anyway, it's hot and very tasty. What a simple easy breakfast. It will be interesting to see if this keeps me feeling full through the morning.

Mid Morning:

Well, I'm halfway through the morning and having a cup of tea but I don't have the usual urge to top up with a snack of some sort. Maybe it's psychological, but so far my cunning plan has been full of cunningness and seems to be working.

Lunchtime:

The morning passed fairly uneventfully and here we are at lunchtime. I can't say that I'm still full from breakfast, I mean after all it was just two eggs, but it seemed to do the trick through the morning. For lunch I have two rolls filled with ham and cheese, a packet of manly crisps, a full sized, non-fun banana and a yoghurt. I've been thinking about crackers covered in sandwich spread. I think that's something from my childhood, I seem to recall my father eating something called "matzos". They were like huge cream crackers and he would smother them with a deep layer of sandwich spread which was a sort of spreadable coleslaw. My mouth is watering thinking about it. I will just have to eat my rolls instead.

Changing the subject slightly, I lost count of how many people talked about the weather today. I know it's meant to be a British thing but for goodness sake, there's really not that much of a variation in the weather here from day to day. Find something else to talk about or the shop keepers of Britain will go off their trolley. Maybe it's a way for people to "talk" without revealing too much about themselves or a way to avoid "proper" conversation.

On the other hand, there is a regular customer who comes in the shop. She never buys a great deal and I think she only really comes here for a chat. The weather is rarely mentioned but she does go into excruciating detail about everything else in her life. I know all about how her ten cats have had various illnesses and how her heating wasn't working properly and how her window cleaner never cleans the corners of the glass. She has a number of friends who all work at the cat protection club, and I know all their marital problems, all their health problems, a few of their National Insurance Numbers, incidents involving false teeth and those special panty pads for ladies of a certain age.

So on reflection, I guess if anyone wants to come and talk to me about the weather, I'm fine with that.

Teatime:

Chicken curry for tea with boiled rice. I'm having it in a bowl again, in fact we all are. A simple but effective idea that as you may remember, reduces portion size. Having said that, my son always struggles to get through his tea whatever size dish he has, it's a fight to get him to eat very much at all. If you had put his food in an egg cup, he would still try and leave half of it.

Garlic and coriander naan breads compliment this meal and are handy for wiping up the sauce. This was a jalfrezi and from a jar so I'm not sure how many calories or how bad this was for me but it was tasty. I read an article that highlighted how much "hidden" fat is in jars of sauce along with too much sugar and salt. Home-made sauces are obviously a better option as you know exactly what's going into it, but time can be an issue in this modern world. In the recipe section at the end of the book is a curry sauce recipe that I often make when my wife goes away (as she doesn't like hot curry).

I'm going to pop out to the local DIY shop as I feel the need to buy a torch. I think it's a man thing. Women don't seem to understand the appeal of holding a big torch in your hands or a really snazzy cordless drill. Yes, OK sometimes we play guns with them or pretend the torch is a light sabre on a frosty or foggy night, but hey, what other pleasure do we get in life. Don't take that away from us too.

Now that I'm here at the DIY store I regret coming here. I do this every time, think it will be a nice trip out and then get cut up in the car park by pensioners who can't even see over the steering wheel, deafened by the screaming kid in the trolley that seems to follow me down every single aisle, and if I ask someone for advice or where a certain product is, I manage to pick the newest newbie or the oldest, deafest, blindest member of staff. Nothing in between.

Anyway, I've got a fair idea of where I'm headed. Oh yeah, torchville baby.

Oh my goodness. I have just seen the biggest torch known to man. I have to have it. It fills me with wonder and merriment. Fifteen, yes count them, fifteen million candle power. I could blind a cat on the moon with this.

I do wonder how they calculate the strength of this. I mean I know one lux is supposed to be the equivalent of the light produced by one candle. But how could you calculate fifteen million candles. By the time you'd lit the last one, the first candle would be burnt out. It would be like painting the Forth Bridge. Actually, I hear they've solved that problem now and will be using a new paint with a laminated finish that will last for a very long time, so we will just have to find a new expression for things that never get finished.

How about "it's like lighting fifteen million candles constantly"? Hmm, it doesn't have quite the same ring about it does it? Anyway, let's lug this behemoth to the checkout and pay for it.

The deed is done. I'm heading home to unwrap this beast and to charge up my sons glow in the dark stickers.....forever!

Day 15- Your Food Diary

Breakfast

Mid Morning

Lunchtime

Teatime

Other snacks

Day 16 - Tuesday - The Lovely Nigella

Breakfast:

Woken up this morning feeling fairly bright and breezy as I had a good deep sleep. It doesn't happen often but last night I certainly went out like a light, helped in no small part by a medium sized glass of vodka and orange. Just the one glass, but I am a bit of a light weight when it comes to alcohol. I certainly wasn't when I was a teenager though. Some friends of mine "worked" with older blokes who would spend all day in the pub, drinking pint after pint, and so that culture of drinking rubbed off onto my friends and then onto me.

We could go out one evening and have anywhere between ten and fifteen pints of lager and still not be drunk. To be honest I don't know how I afforded it, I mean, we were only sixteen. But then beer was cheaper back in 1986. Malibu and coke were all the rage too and I actually liked the taste of that, whereas with beer and lager, I didn't even like it, but it was "cool".

My ignorance was highlighted early on in my drinking days when I went to the barman and asked for two Malibu's in the same glass. He looked suspiciously at me and said "do you mean a double?". We knew where all the pubs were that didn't ask questions about your age and usually got a bag of chips with a pot of curry sauce on the way home to mask the smell of alcohol from our parents. Back then, smoking was allowed in pubs, so we always smelt of that too, not because we smoked but the atmosphere was thick with it. I remember stashing my coat in a shed so that it didn't draw attention to my activities. It hung there for days and still smelt bad.

So, am I hungry? Yes I am. The scrambled egg option yesterday seemed to work very well and kept me full until lunchtime, so I will do the same again today but add in a slice of toast.

Fluffy microwaved scrambled egg on a piece of plain toast and a cup of tea. I feel fairly well fed again and have high hopes of making it through the morning without any snacks.

Lunchtime:
Once again this plan of mine has worked. I did have a cup of tea mid morning but had no urge to ambush the bakery or raid my bag of lunch.

I don't know if it's my imagination but my jeans feel a bit loose. Oh hang on, …..no, they're just broken. What a shame. I was starting to think that by keeping track of what I'm eating, it was making me more conscious of my food intake. I have to say though, that I'm not feeling as bloated as I often do. I still have a face like the full moon, but my belly isn't as puffed out as usual. I wonder if it's because I've had eggs for breakfast and I'm not having wheat cereals, perhaps that's why I'm not bloating as much. This is a possibility as years ago I had an allergy test and it highlighted wheat, cream, butter, emulsion paint and the glue on the back of stamps as things that I was allergic to.

In my early twenties I suffered greatly with what doctors then diagnosed as irritable bowel syndrome. If I had pizza or pasta in any shape or form, my stomach would visibly swell up, I would break out in a sweat and noises like zombies having their toes trodden on would come from my belly. I don't just mean little bubbles and gurgles, we are talking industrial sized noises. Shortly after this I would need to rush to the nearest toilet and explode in a manner that I won't discuss here.

Some people say that irritable bowel syndrome is psychosomatic but that just seems like an uneducated guess or a bit of a cop-out. How could the pizza or pasta or in particular ,cream, make my body react in that way and it all be in my mind? That just doesn't wash with me. Irritable bowel syndrome is a real thing triggered by foods that our body

91

doesn't like or can't tolerate. I've seen (and smelt) the proof.

Over time, the problems seemed to subside and now I can eat pasta's and breads and most wheat based things but cream still sets me off, so as much as possible I try and avoid it, which is a shame because if we go out for a meal, I do like to have a coffee floater at the end. You know the coffee in a glass with a band of cream just floating there on top. Lovely. I will sometimes risk a beef stroganoff, but usually suffer the consequences after.

Right then, a little dig and delve in my carrier bag reveals that today I have cheese and pickle sandwiches with a bag of crisps, a full sized non fun banana and a kit kat.

I'm glad to see that this is a proper bag of crisps. I swear crisps in general are getting smaller and smaller as time goes on and if you ever buy some of the supermarket value packs, there's about four grams of potato slivers masquerading as crisps in there. As for the flavours, well, they must just put the crisps and the flavours in the same building and hope it infuses or something because they rarely taste like what it says on the nasty colourless packaging. But today these are man crisps, thick cut and full of flavour. God bless this company.

Teatime:

I can smell meat of some sort cooking as I enter through the front door. A quick peek in the kitchen tells me that my wife is incinerating some gammon steaks. She does like her meat well done, which is just as well to be honest. I just wish our smoke alarm could differentiate between "cooking" and "towering inferno".

At the end of last year, we went away and stayed in a cottage in Devon. Some friends from Wales came and stayed in a cottage nearby and we did a few trips here and there, Brixham, Paignton, Blackpool Beach and a few other hidden coves around the coast.

One evening, my friends wife invited us around for tea and she had cooked a lovely chicken dinner with all the trimmings, sprouts, broccoli and the all important roast potatoes. We ate, we drank wine, we chatted, we laughed.

To return the favour, I invited them to our cottage a day or so later and experimented on them. Obviously not in a scientific way with probes and test tubes, but in a culinary way. I had seen, some months before, the very curvaceous Nigella Lawson soak a gammon joint in cola overnight and then cook it, or some variation on that. At the time I didn't have the internet available to me or I would have followed her recipe to the letter, however, I had to do it from memory. Having looked it up since, it appears that I needn't have soaked the gammon overnight but could have just cooked it on the day. Never mind. It turned out very nice and as it was a 3KG joint and had been cooked for about ninety four hours, there was enough for everyone and it was tender and juicy and fell off the bone nicely. Of course I topped up everyone's plates with sprouts, roast potatoes and some roast parsnips and then drizzled over the gravy I'd made using the cola/gammon stock.

Everyone seemed to enjoy it apart from my friends two boys who looked at it with horror and then ran off to search the cottage for sweets. My kids, who are a bit more used to being experimented on sat and ate their way through it and then went to join the rampage for sweets. Again we drank wine, we also drank whiskey, we chatted, we laughed and then had another whiskey.

Over the next few days we used up the remains of the ham (apparently according to Nigella, before it's cooked it's called Gammon, and then it becomes ham when it's been cooked). We had ham salad, ham sandwiches, ham risotto, ham, ham, ham. But I'm not complaining, it was lovely.

Anyway, back to my tea. Gammon steaks with the obligatory pineapple ring from a tin sitting on top of it, some boiled potatoes and some mixed vegetables, all washed down with a pint of shandy. Probably not the healthiest meal I've ever had, but I'm sure there's some nutritional value here. I'm not a big fan of boiled potatoes though, they just seem so bland. A swift splurge of red sauce and that problem is resolved.

Supper time:

I've been a bad boy and raided the fridge this evening. I just had a craving for some snacky things and ended up with a glass of wine and some crackers with an assortment of cheeses. Naughty, naughty, evil, fat man.

My foody friend, introduced me, by way of a gift, to a cheese called Ilchester Mexicana, a medium strength cheese with chillies and peppers infused through it. By way of a gift? Yes, we do strange things like that, I in turn have bought her chutneys or pickled peppers in the past too.

Back to this cheese. It is so delicious, it probably has to be one of my favourites. I daren't look at the calories or fat content but it makes beautiful cheese on toast and makes you close your eyes when you eat it and say "oooh".

I've also used it when I make home made pizza. It really adds a depth that wouldn't be there with other plain joyless cheeses.

Full and contented now, so off to bed to see if the cheese gives me nightmares. Yeah, right.

Day 16- Your Food Diary

Breakfast

Mid Morning

Lunchtime

Teatime

Other snacks

Day 17 - Wednesday – Anon.

Breakfast:

Well, I slept like a baby. I mean I had a fairly good sleep, I didn't sleep in a cot and mess myself. What I'm trying to say is that the cheese from last night didn't give me nightmares, but then I didn't expect it to. Such a happy cheese wouldn't know how to make a bad dream let alone a nightmare.

Right then, what shall I have for breakfast? It looks like we are out of eggs so my eggy start to the day can't happen. What a shame. I didn't plan that very well did I?

I think it's going to be toast this morning with chocolate spread. Apparently this chocolate spread is from Belgium. I remember as a child in secondary school, en route to the school we passed an old post office that seemed to specialise in out of date goods. The man behind the counter was huge, and I mean bigger than me and he was always so miserable. He never had a smile for anyone and the only words you would get out of him was the price of the goods you were buying or the occasional bellow of "only two children allowed in the shop at any one time!". His wife was a bit more amiable and always changed her hair to match the current image of the Queen on the latest postage stamps.

My friend Nathan and I thought that we could make some cash by purchasing some of this out of date stock and selling it in school at a profit. We did very well in the summertime by getting the out of date ice-pops for 1p each and selling them down the school field to the hot and sweaty footballers for 5p even though they always tasted a bit vinegary, then we moved on to other goods like a tub of ancient Nutella chocolate spread for 30p and let the kids in the maths class dip their pens in and sold it at 10p per "dip".

Another time they had an offer on garibaldi biscuits and were selling them at 15p for a pound in weight. I did like it back then and made the mistake of eating a whole fifteen pence worth in an afternoon. I cant look at it now without making a huge gulping sound and feeling a little queasy.

We made some good profits on the sweets we sold too. Packets of Pacers were a good seller, they were like Opal Fruits but with a spearmint flavour and green and white stripes. Texans bars didn't sell so well but were a favourite of mine. The money we made probably paid for our beer, although we usually lost it all in a game of "closest to the wall" where a group of you would throw a coin at a wall and see who could get it to land and stay nearest to the wall. The one who achieved this got the money from the other players who's coins were further from the wall.

No Nintendo's or Bluetooth back then. Blimey, I'm making it sound like we didn't have any electronic games at all. I remember being one of the first kids in school to have a hand-held space invaders game and I wanted, but never got, a racing game called demon driver. I'm not sure it was electronic, more mechanical really. I have a very, very vague recollection of it being a sort of motorised roller in a box and you moved a car left and right to avoid obstacles.

Then of course there was the infuriating Simon. A round plastic thing with four coloured quadrants that lit up and beeped. You had to copy the sequence, if you got it wrong it sent a twelve volt shock into your hand. It wasn't meant to, I'd just modified mine to make it more interesting.

I'm going to make a cup of tea to wash this toast down and then I'm off up into my loft to dig around through boxes looking for some drawings I started twenty five years ago.

Mid morning:

Back down again for a drink, a pint of squash, it's thirsty work going through old boxes of stuff and I still haven't found what I'm looking for (as U2 would say on my favourite album of all time The Joshua Tree). Right then, back to it.

Lunchtime:

Going to have an easy lunch of beans on toast today as I don't want to be messing around too long with this. I need to get back to rooting around in the loft for these drawings. About twenty five years ago I was reading a poem and it was written by "Anon", so I got to thinking, who is this Anon bloke? So I came up with a character who had no facial features and whose emotions were mainly portrayed by his body language, therefore he was anonymous.

I bought all the Snoopy and Charlie Brown books I could lay my hands on and started studying them in great detail. The drawings were simple and the messages or stories were succinct and to the point. All this just spurred me on to do some cartoon strips of my own, the sort of thing you might see in a Sunday newspaper, tucked away in the back pages. The only problem was, and remains to be, that I can't draw very well at all. So twenty five years on, the sketches are still stuck in a folder in the depths of my attic. I feel the urge to go through it all again and if I can maybe re-do the drawings to a reasonable standard, I might just go ahead and publish them. Maybe it's just a waste of time but I will be annoyed with myself if I don't give it a try.

The beans are bubbling away nicely here and the bread is in the toaster. I've added a tablespoonful of curry powder to the beans, just to give it a bit of flavour. Very nice and quick to make. A cup of tea will go well with this. Back to the loft soon.

Teatime:

Well it's that time of the day again. It's funny how the day can pass so quickly when you're engrossed in something. I actually did find the folder of drawings and seeing them again has sort of renewed my hope for them. The idea is simple and fairly amusing, it's just the drawings that let them down, so I think that when the springtime comes I shall retreat to my shed, clean it out and turn it into a temporary studio. Then I can re-work the drawings into works of art that even the great Leonardo would smile at. That's Da Vinci, not De Caprio.

Digging around in the fridge I see that my wife has defrosted some chicken pieces and that there is a bag of stir fry vegetables lurking in a puddle of something. Our fridge seems to have sprung a leak or maybe the little drain bit at the back is blocked up. Hmm. Yes, it's blocked, there's a brown thing stuck in it, a little tug and out it pops. I think this used to be a mushroom, or a slug, or a UFO. An Unidentified Fridge Object.

After a quick clean up of the fridge, I then check out the larder cupboard and see that we are very well endowed with a vast range of sauces in jars. Black bean, lemon chicken, sweet and sour, spicy pasta sauce, barbecue sauce, creamy ham, tikka masala, rogan josh, hoi sin, tomato and pepper. I'm feeling like…..black bean sauce would go well with the other bits I've got here.

Hey presto and 30 minutes later I'm serving up chicken and black bean stir fry, washed down with some fizzy elderflower cordial.

Day 17- Your Food Diary

Breakfast

Mid Morning

Lunchtime

Teatime

Other snacks

Day 18 - Thursday - Twenty to Four

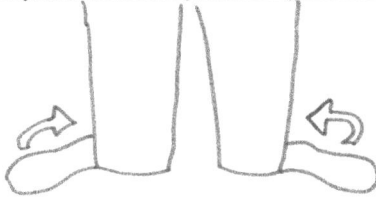

Breakfast:

Slept in a bit longer than I should have (again!) and now I'm rushing to get my son to school and to eat something before heading to the shop. So, I've stuck two bits of bread in the toaster and have a teabag and the milk ready to go in a cup. The toast pops out and while my little man is putting his shoes on I smear some chocolate spread onto the toast and set it aside on a plate.

Back from the school now, which is thankfully only a four minute walk away. Not by accident I'll have you know. All our houses have been close to schools since having the kids, it's always been a criteria when choosing a house and on mornings like this it pays off. I have safely delivered my son to school and I'm back home, all within ten minutes, and there waiting for me is a freshly made cup of tea and two bits of toast with chocolate spread melted into every pore.

Mid Morning:

Managed to avoid snacking so far and just about to have a cup of tea. Not really feeling hungry, just confused. This often happens in the shop when people come in and ask for things that just don't exist like "unsolicited almonds", what they actually wanted was unsulphured apricots but it took quite a while to find that out. Also a lady came in asking for something beginning with "V"??? After about 20 minutes she came to the conclusion that it was Malt extract.

Can you see why I'm confused?

Lunchtime:

Ouch, my knees are playing up. It seems that every day I moan about some new ache or pain. It must be true that when men reach a certain age they turn into "grumpy old men" and their bodies start to fall apart.

My knees are hurting as I have floating cartilage in there, partly caused through a cycling accident and also through my own strange attempt to amuse myself.

The cycling accident goes back to when I used to cycle hundreds of miles per week. A friend who often came with me had planned out a route that would take us from Bristol, England, across the old Severn Bridge and on into Chepstow, South Wales.

Now even before we had started, I was a little apprehensive as it had been a really cold night with temperatures below freezing and there was black ice on the roads, pavements and even up the sides of buildings. As we popped our drinks bottles into the holders on the bike frame and pulled on our pointless, fingerless cycling gloves, my Mum came out of the house and said

"are you sure about this?, it's a bit icy."

"We'll be fine" said my friend Lea trying to sound convincing.

"OK then, be careful, see you later" said Mum.

As we had racing bikes with all the posh bits on, our feet were strapped into the pedals, or at least should have been. Lea, had both feet strapped in, and because of the ice and trying to keep his balance, was weaving back and fore like a snail trying to avoid salt bombs. I thought I would play it safe and only strapped in my right foot, using the other to steady myself. This went on for about the first two miles and then I got fed up doing an impression of a tripod and so strapped in my left foot.

The point of the toe straps is to make the best use of the energy being put into pedalling and even to gain some force from the "up" section of the pedalling action. Usually the only energy produced is when you press down and the bike moves forward. By strapping the toes in, when the back foot is coming round and moving up, you get some pull(and therefore forward momentum). The shoes we had were even moulded to fit into the pedals. Science lesson over.

Now, as much as the toe straps maximised the pedal power, they were a complete pain in the Lycra clad ass when you came to a junction or in particular, traffic lights. That's why the straps were called "quick release" toe straps. In theory, if you reached down and flicked a lever, they would release your feet, or if you took a tumble they would automatically open. We rarely put this to the test but instead would try and time traffic lights so that we could go through without stopping, or if this didn't work, we would do the slow cycle thing and gradually and annoyingly wobble around in front of the queue of cars.

Our route took us through an area called Filton and under what you would probably call an underpass. Lea always saw a hill or an incline as a challenge and would speed on ahead to see how quickly he could get up it. I on the other hand would keep my eyes firmly fixed on the road a few meters in front and try to keep a steady rhythm until I caught up with him and try to ignore the fact that I was on a hill.

This day was no different. Lea had gone on ahead, sped down the road, under the underpass and up the other side like someone had stuck a missile up him. I did my usual steady rhythm and as I got down into the underpass a lorry overtook me and the cab caught my right knee and knocked me into the railings along the left hand side. My left knee and the then the left handlebar knocked one after another railing in a juddering clang and then I toppled down onto my right side under the rear section of the lorry.

As I hit the floor and looked back, I could see one of the huge rear double tyres heading for my face, so I curled my body out of the way and managed to stand up and get to the edge of the road a bit further on past the railings. At that point, I hadn't noticed that my "quick release" toe straps hadn't released quick enough and both my feet were facing the wrong way making me walk like a penguin with piles. Suddenly a wave of nausea swept over me so I sat down with a bump on the pavement being careful not to just drop my bike, I leaned forward and without thinking grabbed hold of each foot and twisted them back into place. I was nearly sick with the pain and the noise my knees had made and so I lay down flat on the pavement and must have blacked out for a short time. The lorry never stopped and I don't know if he even knew he had hit me. Nowadays with the streets littered with CCTV camera's I think I could have called him to account, but back then it was a rarity to see a camera.

The next thing I know, Lea has realised that I'm not behind him and has come back to see what's going on and found me passed out. So we sat there for a bit, had a Mars bar, a bag of prawn cocktail crisps and a drink, and then got back on the bikes and carried on to Chepstow. How manly and how convenient that this happened near to a newsagent heavily stocked with prawn cocktail crisps.

Along the way we amused ourselves by timing how long it would take for our spit to go from the walkway of the old Severn Bridge to the water below. I seem to remember it depended on the consistency of the flob and the direction of the wind. They don't teach you that in school today, in fact as far as I can tell, they don't teach you anything at all, just send you home with a load of homework because the teacher was too busy on Facebook in class.

So that was the first time I had damaged my knees. They should have been checked out by a doctor and put back into joint by a medic rather than a roadside DIY job. The second time was in the flat in Cardiff. For some strange reason one day, I just wondered how far round I could get my feet from the normal position(which we shall call 12 'O' clock).

I was comfortable with them at 10 to 2, so I moved them around a bit more and even a quarter to 3 felt reasonably bearable and I know you're sat there now moving your feet round. The trouble started when I moved them to 20 to 4. Something in each knee clicked and for a brief moment I was about an inch taller and then the pain set in. I had to fall to the ground and slowly and excruciatingly try and twist them back to 12 'O' clock.

Eventually I got them back in, but since those two occasions I have had trouble with bits of cartilage floating around and getting caught under the knee cap. Sometimes there's a real burning sensation when I walk down the stairs, not up, just down. The doctors have said that I could have an operation to remove the floating bits, but that it would probably do more harm than good, so I've just left it for now.

So in between moaning about the pain and serving customers I have checked my bag and it appears that today I have chicken sandwiches, a bag of thick cut crisps and a pear. That makes a change from one of those annoying bananas. The pear feels soft and noisy. How can a pear feel noisy? Well, when they feel this soft, you know that when you take a bite, you will have to save your chin and t-shirt from the juice by doing a great big noisy slurp. Let me try….. Yes, a very noisy pear. Nice though.

Teatime:

Oh boy. What a long day, and what a lot of strange people coming through the door asking bizarre questions. A few requests for Viagra today. No we don't sell it, yes there are some herbal remedies that may help with the circulation in that general vicinity, but in the meantime, here's two lolly sticks and an elastic band. You work it out.

Thankfully, as I'm not in the mood to cook anything and as my wife is home before me on a Thursday, I've arrived home to the smell of roasting chicken, and sure enough there it is, roast chicken thighs, cauliflower cheese and sweet corn with some potato croquettes. A glass of rose lemonade and a bread roll complete this meal and leave me feeling like I need a snooze. Not a chance, as dad, the homework solver, is called into action for the millionth time and also used for multiple donkey rides around the living room. No wonder my knees are mashed. You'd think my wife would have grown out of donkey rides by now, wouldn't you?

I hope to sit quietly later and watch mindless TV.

Day 18- Your Food Diary

Breakfast

Mid Morning

Lunchtime

Teatime

Other snacks

Day 19 - Friday - Sticky Knuckles

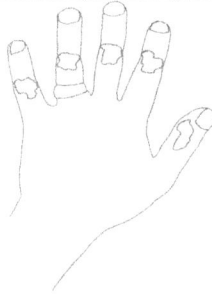

Breakfast:

I've got today off again, so I should, in theory, have more time to make myself a proper breakfast, but as usual, I've slept a bit longer than is practical, so I find myself joining my son for some wholly un-nutritious cereal and a cup of tea as we are sat watching the Pink Panther cartoon for a while before the mad dash to get dressed and take him to school. A nice way to start the day but I now have the Pink Panther music in my head, and I have a feeling it will be there all day long.

Lunchtime:

Well, the morning was fairly event free, a trip to the bank to let the bank manager know that I was still alive. A quick visit to a discount store to get some wire and electronic bits for a project I've been instructed to do by my son. He wants me to dismantle a wind up torch and insert the LEDs or bulbs into small lamp holders and place them at strategic points on his bedroom ceiling. The thinking behind this, and this is his thinking, not mine, is that if there is a power cut or electricity prices get too silly, he will be able to wind up the dynamo and have light in his room. In some ways I admire his resolve to be prepared and to have an alternative plan, on the other hand, what sort of world have I brought this kid into where an 8 year old has to worry about rising electricity prices. It always surprises me how much he takes in, even when you think he's not listening, he's soaking it all up.

An easy ham and cheese sandwich is what I'm going to have for lunch with some pickle. Not pickle from a glass jar where you have to prod around with your knife and get sticky knuckles, but pickle from a squeezy bottle.

I'd sit quietly and enjoy this but that damn pink panther music is still in my head.

Teatime:

I've been pottering in the garden this afternoon, making plans for when the weather is better. I've been surprised by how many sets of ladders I seem to have accumulated over the years. I probably have every set that I ever bought apart from my first ones. They were a light aluminium pair that were from some DIY superstore and they did the job up until I bent them.

Yes, I bent some ladders. Not through being too heavy, because this was when I first started window cleaning. I had a particularly nasty round in a place called Llantwit Major. It was one of those estates that you could imagine being built by a robot as every house was the same and no love or care had gone into the design. Some of the smaller, one bedroom houses were not much bigger than my van, but generally they were three bedroom semi detached houses all with a window above an impossibly steep roof and with gardens landscaped so that a ladder couldn't be placed safely anywhere near the house. When it rained, the estate became waterlogged and your ladder could sink two feet into a lawn.

Because of this many of the customers didn't want me stepping on their grass or putting the ladder on the it, so the upstairs windows in those places just got left. Nowadays you tend to see window cleaners armed with a long pole with a brush on the end, spraying out de-ionised water. That way they don't have any ladder work, which is better for them, but you can't beat cleaning a window the proper way and wiping the sills so it doesn't drip everywhere. Still, health and safety are putting their oar in and trying to get rid of ladders all together.

Anyway, one such house had a window that hadn't been cleaned for a while and as I'd made such a good job of the rest of the house, this one window stood out like a sore thumb. So, I thought I'd give it a go. It was a sunny day, so the roof I would have to cross wasn't slippery, the ground was dry too, so I thought I would risk it. Up the ladder I went and as my feet got up by the gutter line the feet of the ladder slipped away. The ladder dropped down and as it went, my feet got caught under the rungs. I fell with all the acrobatic grace of a noodle. In an instant I was laying on my back on top of the ladder with my feet mangled under the rungs weighed down by my own body weight. I'd made such a clatter you would have expected the whole neighbourhood to come and see. But no-one was home at this house and the next door neighbour just glanced out of his window, gave me a strange look and then went back to watching the snooker.

I had fallen about twelve feet and landed on my back and I was a bit winded, so I lay there for about twenty minutes catching my breath and watching the clouds roll by, the curtains next door twitching now and then. When I eventually had enough oxygen in my lungs to have the energy to extricate myself from the aluminium wreck, my ladder looked like the letter "K" laying on its back with a me-sized dent in it. I don't know if I broke any bones that day but twelve years later I can still kick a brick wall with the big toe on my right foot and not feel a thing.

The really annoying part was that the people in that house moved the following month and never paid me. I packed up for the day after my accident and on the way home popped into a friends house as I remembered they had some pain relief spray and I also wanted some sympathy.

I got the spray.

For tea today my wife has made chicken pie with mashed potato and peas, all smothered in thick beefy gravy.

Day 19- Your Food Diary

Breakfast

Mid Morning

Lunchtime

Teatime

Other snacks

Day 20 - Saturday - A Rash

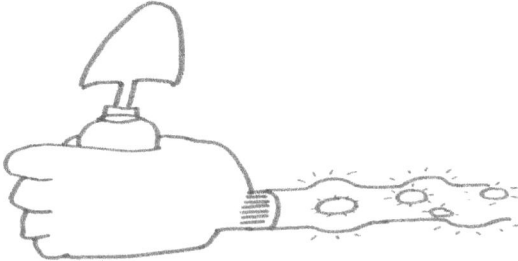

Breakfast:

Got up when I felt like it today, so no rushing around. Popped into my daughter's room to pinch her I-pod as I feel like having some music on, but I got sidetracked. She has two, full length mirrored doors on her wardrobe and as I walked past I spotted stretch marks.

Shock, horror. Actually, neither. I knew I had them, but sometimes you forget, only to be reminded by a chance encounter with a mirror. These are on my biceps and presumably because I haven't been doing weight training for a long while. Once upon a time, I had a fine set of arms, big and inflated and would happily wear vest tops and do my Bruce Willis impersonation. But now, my sleeves are a little longer.

I've still got a set of weights out in the garden, but they are the plastic ones filled with concrete and as they have been left out in frosts and snow, the plastic has cracked and the concrete drops off when I pick them up. It somehow seems symbolic because I feel exactly the same, I'm cracking up and bits are dropping off of me.

Well, now I've completely forgotten what I was doing, so I will head downstairs and have a cup of tea and two pieces of buttered toast.

Lunchtime:

I've been in the garden trying to make the most of the winter months and hack back some of the bushes and trees that are trying to take over

111

my garden before they fully erupt into life again through the spring and summer. It seemed like a good idea at the time but now I'm not so sure as most of my body is scratched and cut and I've come out in a rash on my arms. I believe this proves what I've always thought. I'm allergic to gardening.

A fact that I have been trying to convince my father of for the last forty years, or at least since I was old enough to hold a spade without chewing it.

It's not like I don't see the point of gardening or being self sufficient, it's just not my main interest in life and I don't intend to dedicate the entire garden or every waking hour to arable farming or agronomy. I do have a greenhouse and have set aside some raised beds to plant sprouts, potatoes, onions, chillies, peppers, tomatoes and strawberries. So it's not like I'm not having a go.

I don't think gardening is in my blood, my mother, sister, grandparents, aunties, uncles and cousins are all allergic to gardening as well, so where my fathers fascination with soil comes from, I don't know.

The most fun I ever had in a garden was cutting the grass in France in a gite that my mother had rented. It was the first and last ever holiday we've all had together. My sister and her husband and their year old son, my Mum and dad, me, my wife and our one year old daughter all stayed in a musty, spider filled, dark, damp barn masquerading as a Gite.

The journey across was awful, the ferry was thrown about like a leaf in the wind and to make things worse we had opted for the long ferry journey in favour of a shorter drive when we arrived. I tend to get sea sick sitting in the bath, so being confined to a ship rolling and pitching through stormy seas did upset me a bit and I was rather sick, in fact after seven hours of this nausea I was left as a pale and drawn husk of a man.

Even the staff on the boat were retching over the side which is never a good sign. But my brother in law seemed unaffected by this, as if he was able to zone out and exist in his own little sea-sick proof bubble. We were glad he did this as he was able to look after both the babies.

Anyway, after we had landed in France and found our way through overgrown country lanes, we arrived at what looked like a derelict barn, but sure enough the name plate matched the details on the information sheet we had been given. "Les Menhirs". I have to say, there's an awful lot of blokes in France called Les.

The key was in the door, so we pushed it open with a creak, or it may have been our hands, and a flurry of moths escaped shouting "Vive la France" as they headed straight for the sun. It was then that the damp smell hit us like a frying pan to the face. For the next few hours we all pitched in and cleaned up the place and made it a bit more habitable.

During this cleaning and exploring time we came across a green metal garden shed and as we opened the double doors, there shining in all it's metal glory was a ride-on lawn mower, you know the ones, like a midgets tractor. The keys were in it and the grass was long, so we all took turns to carve up the grass and have races, doing circuits of the garden and winning bottles of bier blanc for the fastest lap. That evening I made tiriyaki beef, we drank beer and we tried to sleep with our mouths shut and one eye open, looking out for spiders.

I'm not really very hungry but I've certainly had enough of gardening and it's started to rain and I don't have a ride-on mower, three good reasons to stop, so I've come in and I'm going to make cheese and pickle sandwiches and have a cup of tea.

Teatime:

As my wife is away with my son today, my daughter has been set with the task of providing a meal for us. I've had to pop out for a bit, but returning home I see that the house hasn't been burned down, and no acrid stench coming from the kitchen. All good signs.

So let's see what delight she has conjured up. I have to say my expectations are not high as the "cookery" lessons she has had in school so far this term have consisted of making a fruit salad, cooking a pizza and chopping a tomato. I mean, come on! How mind numbingly unhelpful. I'm sure most of the kids already knew how to chop fruit into a bowl, or how to open the oven door and put a pizza in. When I was in school we made stuff from scratch, sponges, fruit cakes, scones, quiches, even pasta, bread and pizza bases, but now they seem to just point them in the direction of a microwave and assume that it will be a great help to the kids in their future lives.

Anyway, I am happy to smell something good coming from the kitchen, and lo and behold, meatballs and spaghetti in a tomatoey pasta sauce, hot, well cooked and tasty. Well done Michaela.

A pint of orange squash lubricates the whole meal and we sit and chat about boys for a while, her singing their praises and me putting her off.

Day 20 - Your Food Diary

Breakfast

Mid Morning

Lunchtime

Teatime

Other snacks

Day 21 - Sunday - Farting on a Westie

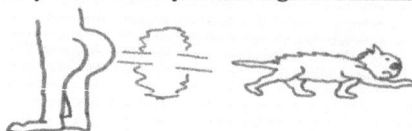

Breakfast:

The nice thing about Sundays is not having to rush and so that gives me a bit more time to prepare something for breakfast instead of the usual rush to grab a packet of cereals or have nothing at all, so this morning I am going to have two pieces of wholemeal bread and two poached eggs with a cup of tea. For a minute there I thought I might fancy a cup of coffee but when I opened the coffee jar and took a sniff, my bowels recoiled and it put me off.

My only problem with poached eggs is that when I make them, they always seem to explode off in different directions and end up looking like spilt milk in outer space. Once as an anniversary "treat" I stayed in Thornbury castle, my wife would have loved it.

For breakfast I ordered the poached egg on toast. I have no idea how they did it, but it was the most perfectly smooth white with the thickest and yet runniest yellow ever, oozing out as I pressed it with my fork.

I may have to invest in an egg poacher. I'm not sure how they work, I've only ever glanced at them in passing some hardware stores, but they must be an improvement on my efforts. I think that maybe I have been poaching them in too much water. I generally fill a pan to about three or four inches of water, but someone suggested to me that I use a shallow pan, like a frying pan and just use enough water to cover the egg. Also fresh eggs are a must.

Yet again, my efforts have resulted in what looks like egg soup with lots of straggly eggy spider legs. They taste nice although I wouldn't win a prize for elegance here. My son has decided not to try any but my daughter has already polished off half of my breakfast.

Off to the shed I think to sort through a pile of old documents that need shredding or saving. Hopefully the egg (back to the protein for breakfast idea again) will keep me going until lunchtime.

Lunchtime:

A pigs leg is what we are having today. That thought alone will make some vegetarians wince, but we are all carnivores here and like to chow down on some flesh and gnaw the bones. Having said that, pork isn't top of my list when it comes to meat. There's a porky taste that I'm not too keen on. I know that sounds obvious, but it's like some fish taste more fishy than others. There seem to be different flavours from different parts of the pig. The gammon I cooked in cola had a very nice meaty flavour, but already the smell coming from the kitchen isn't giving me much hope. It's a bit like you would imagine a morgue to smell on a hot day.

I think the reason we are having this is because it was on offer in the supermarket. As good a reason as any. I have the urge to sharpen a knife and carve the old fashioned way rather than plugging in the electric knife. What lazy so and so invented that anyway. My son will be pleased if I save electric too.

Well, there it is, a pigs leg, minus the trotter, surrounded by roast potatoes, cabbage, carrots and parsnips. A dollop of apple sauce, a bottle of white wine and we are ready to go.

Teatime:

We are all still full from our lunch so for tea we are having cucumber sandwiches. How very summery in the depths of winter. The last time I had cucumber sandwiches for tea was about 23 years ago at my wife's grandmothers house. It was a Saturday afternoon ritual that I got dragged into. Apparently it was something that they had done for years and as I would go to Cardiff and stay with my outlaws when I was courting, they took me along with them. My wife wasn't allowed to not go, and as the point of my visit was to see her, I had to go along with them.

The cucumber sandwiches had been cut so small by her grandmother that you could almost be forgiven for thinking that somewhere Ken and Barbie were cursing their bad luck at losing their picnic. Along with these minuscule morsels were tiny butterfly cakes and tea in gold trimmed bone china cups with handles that you couldn't get your finger in, balanced on matching saucers. There were also Welsh cakes that had spent a little too long on the hob and looked more like burgers than a cakey nibble.

We were always so hungry afterwards that we would often head off into the local village to the Top Gun chip shop and get a bag of chips and a pot of curry sauce and take them back to the outlaws house. There we would be greeted by their West Highland Terrier called Heidi. I obviously hadn't seen her as a puppy but I think she was meant to be white and fluffy, however by the time I was introduced to her she was more off white and matted and had the annoying habit of always being where your next step was going to be. Not at all like the cute white one on the advert that finds your car keys or brings your slippers to you.

Another annoying habit she had was to lick my face in the mornings. I would usually sleep in a sleeping bag on the floor in the front room of the outlaws house and she would try to climb in. If I tried to stop her or push her away, she would growl and once or twice gave me a bit of a nip. After two years of this, I got fed up with what I saw as an invasion of my face. I'd seen that dog sat licking her bits and so I wasn't overjoyed to have her sharing the same tongue with my face or trying to force her way into the sleeping bag. The addition of meaty bad breath didn't help the situation and so one day when she was wedging her way into the sleeping bag and made her way down to my feet, I summoned up a sizeable fart and let rip. I quickly got out of the sleeping bag and folded the top over, temporarily trapping the meaty breathed monster inside. A little later I let her out. She never did it again.

Some years later she drowned in the garden pond, I wonder if it may have been a suicide.

Day 21 - Your Food Diary

Breakfast

Mid Morning

Lunchtime

Teatime

Other snacks

Day 22 - Monday - "No Starters?!".

Breakfast:

Woken up feeling ravenous so I think I will have some waffles. I haven't had these for ages and I think the last time I did, my sister in law fried them in a pan and stuck fried eggs on top. This morning though I will just pop them in the toaster. They're small and joined together in pairs, so I am having four of them and putting butter on them while they are still hot. Mmm they smell good. Right then, a cup of tea should help.

Wow, they taste nice but are very heavy and stick to the roof of your mouth. The cup of tea is a necessity to help remove them, either that or a chisel.

Need to step up the pace a bit now as time is moving on.

Mid Morning:

It's been a fairly uneventful morning. The usual few early bird customers who pop in, get their prunes, figs or other bowel friendly fruits and then scurry off home before the mad rush begins. The 'mad rush' hasn't happened for a while, so they are getting up early for no good reason. A senseless and futile crime if you ask me.

We did have one lady come in selling bracelets for a cause we had never heard of, the Blaketon Lemming Appeal. First of all, where's Blaketon. Second, Lemmings? And third, why would I want to appeal to a lemming?

There was something about her that didn't ring true even though she had a tray of rubbery bracelets with "Save a Lemming today" stamped on them. Do we even get lemmings in this country?

We didn't buy any. I don't even like lemmings and I certainly don't like wearing bracelets. Probably the only time I ever did wear one was when we stayed at an all inclusive hotel in Spain. You had to wear it to prove that you were a guest and that you hadn't just wandered in off of the street looking for free grub.

It wasn't even a comfortable band of rubber but a nasty, sharp, stiff plastic one that was just tight enough to cause chafing when sand from the beach got underneath it, but not big enough to remove for bathing, sleeping or letting blood flow through to your fingers.

The hotel receptionist who fitted it on my wrist had a nasty gleam in his eye as he clicked shut the un-openable plastic clasp which was just so placed as to press on some obscure, negative acupressure point, inducing migraines and hallucinations.

Having access to food and drinks twenty four hours a day certainly added to the appeal of the holiday, but having our withered hands amputated at the end of the week took the shine off of the whole thing.

Actually, the food at the all inclusive hotel wasn't that great, the same old things being served day after day. Big signs up promising wonderful new dishes and stunning desserts all failed to deliver. One sign promised Chinese rice, but it turned out to be about as Chinese as Mickey Rooney. There must be some hotel manual with a section called "Large scale Chinese cuisine on a budget" which asserts that by adding chopped spring onions to a dish, you will make it Chinese. The spring onions were actually a welcome addition to the rice which had presumably been boiling since the Ming Dynasty.

The next night we were promised Indian rice. So, a quick flick through the manual to "Large scale Indian cooking on a budget" and here we are told that adding sultanas and enough yellow food colouring to put a banana farm to shame should do the trick. Up until this day I had never produced a yellow poo, but there it was in the pan, mocking me as I tried and tried to flush it into oblivion.

During our stay in Spain, we felt a little adventurous and took the risk of getting a bus to an unknown destination. I say unknown because nobody knew where it was going, even the driver was a bit vague about the route and reversed back a few times to turn down roads he had missed. The bus seemed to be taking the gangland route and drove through parts of town where we hoped the windows on the bus were bullet-proof.

I often wished that my knowledge of Spanish was better so that I could first of all converse with the driver and perhaps help him find his way again, and also to be able to read the signs. One sign that bemused me, simply said "Manneken -Pis". I've heard of weeping statues, so I guess this could just be a progression from that. I found out later it was a beer.

Another sign was for ice cream from a company called "Frigo". Would you eat ice cream from a company called Frigo? Hmm, I think not.

Some of the more common signs were a bit misleading too, for example if you walked through a door labelled "Salida" you might hope to end up in a big field of leafy vegetables, but it just means "exit". The graphics can also be a little confusing to those of a simpler state of mind. My wife at one point saw the graphic on an emergency door showing two hands pushing the bar to unlock it. "Oh look" she said, "they have a weights room."

Looking on the bright side, if there ever was an emergency or a fire, she will probably be found in the weights room looking a little bewildered.

Lunchtime:

Lunchtime is here, thank goodness. I don't know what's wrong with me today, I feel like I could eat a horse. Strangely enough, that's one meat I haven't knowingly tried. I don't have a problem with it though, I'd have a nibble. I have sandwiches today with ham, not the freshly sliced ham you get from a deli where they wrap it lovingly in paper for you and present it to you like they are returning something they gratefully borrowed, but the reformed lips, elbows, knuckles and eyelids that they press into squares and plop into a plastic wrapper. The lack of flavour is counteracted with some rather nice Bavarian smoked cheese slices. I also have a yoghurt that the manufacturer couldn't be bothered blending with a flavour, so I have to do it for them, tipping it in and stirring it up, a chocolate biscuit and a Braeburn apple.

Oh, damn it! A large section of my sandwich just decided to leap out and take a dive for the floor. Much to my dads disgust I retrieved and ate it. I hate to see food wasted. I know some people use the "five second rule" whereby they say that if food hasn't been in contact with the floor for more than five seconds, it's OK to eat it. If you've ever seen the show Mythbusters on the Discovery channel, there was an episode where they debunked that myth. There was no more bacteria on a piece of food that had been on the floor for thirty seconds than one that had been there for five seconds.

Anyway, my mother and I have our own rule, if it can be picked or scraped up, it's fair game. My dad would rather sell his own mother than eat food off of the floor.

Good job it's my sandwich then.

Teatime:

Right then, time for a dad and daughter moment. As my daughter and I are the only ones who like Indian food, I am taking her for a curry at a local eatery called The Tamarind. I've only just thought to do this and told her we are going to get a curry. In her mind she thinks we are just popping to a takeaway and so she is slumming it a bit in her old "comfy" clothes. I also haven't gone overboard on dressing up.

It's suddenly dawned on my daughter that we are eating in a restaurant and she is mortified that she is dressed like a bag lady. I tell her no one will even notice.

As we walk in through the main door, the eyes of the surprisingly small man greeting customers widen and he looks us up and down. "Can I assume you haven't made a reservation?" he says.

"That's right" I say, "a table for two please."

"Please wait here Sir while I discuss this with the management."

My daughter pulls her jumper up over her face and prays for the ground to open up and swallow her. The man returns and says "follow me please" and leads us to a table obscured from the view of other customers. He pulls a few potted trees around behind us, forming a sort of dense wooded area at the back of the restaurant.

My daughter and I have in fact eaten here before and also managed to dress for the occasion. On our first visit, we discovered, much to the dismay of our non-elasticated trousers that the portions served here are fairly generous, so this time around we decided to just have a main course. I'm sure too that my daughter felt the less time spent eating, the quicker we could go home and hide. The little man came back and asked if we were ready to order, so I ordered two Chicken Tikka Biriyanis, a Peshwari naan and a Keema naan.

"No starters!!!?" said the little man gasping in horror.

"No thank you" I said.

He gave me a look of total hatred and snatched away the cutlery that was to be used with the starters, made his way through the dense thicket surrounding us and flounced off to the kitchens.

Twenty minutes later, another small man arrived and put a glowing hot piece of metal on the table between us, "be careful" he helpfully suggested, "it's very hot."

"oh really?" we said, as our eyelashes turned to ash.

The first little man came back carrying our food and slid it down in front of us. He just about managed to choke out the word "enjoy" and scurried off. Once again the portions were certainly generous and the Biriyani was piping hot from sitting on the portable volcano we had been given. We ordered a coke and a lemonade, ate the food, chatted about all kinds of things ranging from make-up to cooking and flashers over the local common. Then I went and paid yet another small man and we headed home, full, but not too bloated. Even though we'd upset the owners by not having a starter, our bellies were thanking us.

The next time we go there, we should make more of an effort. Who knows, I might even invest in some bigger trousers. I believe that when men get to a certain age they stop buying trousers and head to the section of the clothes shop labelled "Slacks". I'm not at that stage yet and to be honest the word itself goes through me. My nan used to call a dress a "frock" and that always seemed wrong too.

Right then, we are home now and my daughter has rushed into the house still suffering from the utter shame of being seen in public dressed as some kind of country bumpkin.

She will get over it I'm sure. It's all part of life's rich experience.

Day 22 - Your Food Diary

Breakfast

Mid Morning

Lunchtime

Teatime

Other snacks

Day 23 - Tuesday – Kissing David Bellamy.

Breakfast:

Frosted cereals this morning, a ruddy great big bowl of them and a cup of tea. Watching a bit of the Mr Bean cartoon with my son as we eat. He's a little anxious about going to school today as he is getting pushed around a bit. He's one of the smaller children in the class and there are some boys that seem to enjoy pushing him over or getting him in headlocks. I never had that problem in school as I was one of the biggest in the class. If there was ever trouble it was often one of the smaller kids trying to assert themselves or pretending that they didn't have a chip on their shoulder about their lack of stature. However, in my son's class it's working the opposite way round. I've shown him a few good moves for getting out of headlocks and how to temporarily disable an assailant by landing a well aimed elbow, foot or knee into a stomach or ball bag but he's such a gentle soul and worries about getting told off by the teachers and hurting the other children. I've tried to explain that the staff seem to be oblivious but he's having none of it. Maybe that makes him a better person than me. Good lad.

Maybe he will have a massive growth spurt when he's older and flatten them or on a less physical note, maybe he will end up as their probation officer.

Justice will prevail.

Mid Morning:

Had a lady in today asking for Black Goulash. Straight away I knew
she meant Black Cohosh which can be used to help relieve hot flushes
or night sweats, but it's fun to play along and wind them up a bit, so for
a while I went and searched through the food section muttering about
Hungarian food and then gave the lady a recipe for Serbian bean stew
called pasulj (recipe listed at the back).
I have to amuse myself this way or the drudgery will make me pull my
eyes out. A cup of tea helps too.

Lunchtime:

Today I have chicken sandwiches, a bag of cheap nasty supermarket
brand crisps that are about one atom thick, an apple and a yoghurt.
You'd think that I should be a little sentimental about eating chicken as
we kept them when I was a child, although I don't ever remember eating
them. As far as I know, we just kept them to have fresh eggs, unless my
parents kept the dreadful truth from me and I did in fact eat one of them.

We had a variety of chickens, not that I can remember all of them. One
was called a Rhode Island Red, another was called a Polish something
or other. She was funny because she had a great big bush of feathers on
her head that covered her eyes like a big feather afro. How she could
walk around without bumping into things I will never know. I
imaginatively called her Polish.

My favourite though was a bantam, I have no idea what breed or
flavour she was but she developed a strange habit of flying up and
sitting on my arm when I walked into the chicken coop, so I called her
Hawk and I would proudly show off to any friends that came to visit.
The joy of this was lost a bit when she cacked down my sleeve.

We also had Aylesbury ducks and my dad built a great big duck pond
for them to splash about in. I thought they were brilliant and they
always seemed so happy, almost laughing as they quacked and splashed.
Dad however got rid of the pond about a week after he had built it as he
said they were too messy. Too messy for what?, it's not like we were
taking them to a wedding or anything, and they gave us huge eggs

128

which according to my mother are really good for making sponge cakes. Nevertheless the pond became a memory and actually, now that I think about it, so did the ducks. I wonder where they went. I don't think I will ask though.

I remember at some point in my childhood seeing one of the ducks (called Ducky) pushing their way into a bramble bush and then being stuck in there. This particular duck always seemed to waddle around with another one called Quacky. Don't laugh, I was only about seven. Anyway, when Ducky was well and truly stuck in the middle of the bramble bush, she seemed to be calling to Quacky for help and before we could do anything about it she wedged her way into the bush too.

I was devastated and had to wait until dad came home to try and free them. The problem was that they had got into such a state and as he chopped the bushes back and got nearer to them, they panicked and cut themselves to ribbons on the thorns. It really upset me to hear their distressed quacks. I think I cried for a long time and dad had to put them out of their misery. We had a lovely roast dinner the next day.

Hmm.

Teatime:

My Mum said today that she had made a game pie recently containing partridge and rabbit. My dad hated it but that's no surprise, he hates anything that's more adventurous than sausage and mash. But it got me thinking, I've never had either and I know my son would be mortified if he thought I'd eaten a fluffy bunny. I've never eaten horse or goat either.

When I worked in a small job centre in Cardiff Bay (the posh name for the docks) there was a large Somali community and they would often cook goat for their meals. I wish I'd asked where the goats came from because I just don't know where you'd get it. I've checked in my local butchers and they looked at me a bit gone off. Maybe a farm shop could help.

Yet again, you'd think that I would be adverse to eating something that I once considered as a pet. We had a nanny goat when I was about nine years old called Heidi and she had three kids. I remember her giving birth in a small coal shed, my Mum has photographs of the occasion where the flash on the camera has lit up a bag of placenta hanging from the rear of the goat. This may explain my phobia of red balloons.

The kids were really cute and made little bleating noises, I even remember taking one to school and everyone thought it was a lamb. A great deal of amusement was caused too when Heidi decided to poo on the playground, much to the horror of Mr Gwinn the caretaker. Generally she was very well behaved. We used to exercise her by taking her for a walk on a lead around the block. I'm not even sure that's legal, but like I said she was well behaved and if she wanted a poo she would walk over to the gutter and do it there so that all the little steaming nuggets would plip down into the drain below. If we could train a goat to do that, you dog owners should sit up and take note.

A week or two after the kids were born an acquaintance of my parents came to see them. "Ooh can I hold one" he said.

"They're a bit wriggly" said dad.

"I'll hold on tight, don't worry"

So this man picked up one of the baby goats and it struggled and kicked and he dropped her. A snapping noise split the air and then a shriek of pain. The baby goat had broken her neck and was screaming.

"Oh" said the goat killer.

He is still known as the goat killer to this day, thirty one years later. I don't think we even got a "sorry" from him. Dad had to quickly put the goat out of it's misery out of sight of me and my three year old sister. The goat killer got his coat and went. I don't think he's been back since but if he did, I would force him to sit on the goat skin stool we seem to have acquired.

We had a dog called Henry for a while. The only reason I thought of that was because I'd said about the goat going to toilet in the gutter, we'd trained Henry to do the same. He was a slightly psychotic Schnauzer who would bark at anything and everything and would howl all night. I remember sitting with him one night in the small hours of the morning because I felt sorry for him. He did stop howling then. It seemed he needed constant company. I know some humans like that.

Eventually, as we couldn't provide the constant company Henry needed, we gave him to a retired gentleman who lived in a field or something. Apparently he had a marvellous time running round like a mad thing barking at hedgerows or anything that rustled until one day he got run over and squashed by a milk float. The dog, not the old man.

A few years later we thought we'd try again and bought another Schnauzer and called him Oscar. This one was a lot quieter and had the good sense to not be under your feet as you walked, he trained easily, could sit, fetch, beg, roll over and lie down. He had the biggest eyebrows I had ever seen on a dog and a bit of a wind problem. This had it's advantages. If you had quietly chuffed your buttocks, it was common sense to blame the dog and have him put outside. One Saturday morning when my sister was still asleep I picked Oscar up, an action that seemed to trigger the farting and sat him on her face. I think she dreamt that she was kissing David Bellamy but she quickly woke up when she realised that his breath was like a dogs bum.

I've never seen anyone wash their face for so long.

Some time later as my parents were both working and couldn't devote a great deal of time to Oscar, he was donated to my grandparents. My grandfather thought it was wonderful but my nan wasn't too sure. Initially she had some sort of phobia about touching him and would only smooth him whilst wearing gloves. In time this changed and she loved him to bits, even letting him sit in Gramps chair after he had died, a privilege denied most humans.

OK, time to eat. Tonight for tea we are having cottage pie, I suppose that's as near as I will get to goat today. We also have green beans, thick gravy and a pint of shandy.

Day 23 - Your Food Diary

Breakfast

Mid Morning

Lunchtime

Teatime

Other snacks

Day 24 - Wednesday - Hot Chocolate and a Tart.

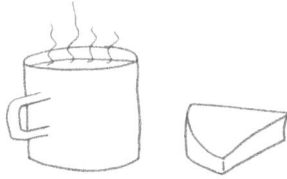

Breakfast:

Woken to find a light covering of snow blanketing the gardens and streets. Not unusual I suppose in January, but I'm sure this wasn't forecast. I'm not in the shop today so I have time to make a more elaborate breakfast, so I'm going with a few croissants, chocolate spread, some pieces of ham and a hot chocolate. Very continental and puts me in mind of my snowboarding trips.

On the first trip I went to stay with a friend, Nathan who lives in Grenoble, France and not too far from the mountains. He was originally from Bristol and we grew up together, went through the same schools and generally spent a lot of our adolescence doing what kids do. I remember clearly that he always had a knack for locating and stepping in doggy doo on the way to school and became an expert at getting it out of the grooves in his shoes. I'm fairly convinced that he invented the moonwalk through this process.

In preparation for this trip I had scoured eBay and found a snowboard and boots for a good price, I had a ski jacket, goggles and gloves so I was already looking the part.

In order not to look like a complete amateur I had gone to a dry ski slope in Cardiff and had an hours lesson. Initially this seemed like a good idea but on reflection it probably taught me very little at all. If you've ever been on a dry ski slope you will know that it is like an oversized welcome mat, the prickly coconut mats that most of us wipe muddy feet on when entering our porches and distinctly lacking in welcome.

Compare that spiky, hard, unforgiving surface with soft, freshly fallen snow and you will see what I'm saying. The only similarity is that a snowboard can move across both surfaces at varying speeds, and in the early stages of your snowboarding experience you will most likely find that you have no control whatsoever over those speeds.

After arriving at Grenoble airport and catching a bus the twenty minute trip to Grenoble train station where I was to be picked up, I rang my friends house and then waited for his wife to pick me up. We then drove the short distance to their home and I settled into the guest room they had kindly prepared for me. I had met their children some years before and so they felt comfortable enough to greet me with a series of random beatings and rifling through my luggage looking for interesting gadgets. The two children are fluent in French and English, which I always find impressive. Children's brains are like sponges and in this country we waste the opportunity to utilise that by waiting until kids are twelve to teach them languages.

After a few days when the work schedule of my friend allowed, we drove up into the mountains surrounding Grenoble and I was sent off to a ticket office to get a pass for the ski lift. I say ticket office, it was more of a wooden hut. As I practised my broken school boy French on the man in the hut and spent 20 Euros or so on a ticket that would last me the afternoon, I looked around to see my friend and his boys approaching people in the car park. As it turned out, they had perfected the art of spotting who was leaving the slopes for the day and talked them into handing over the lift passes that would run out by the end of the day, thus saving their family numerous Euros.

My friends wife, as a teacher, had a whole bundle of school work with her to mark and grade and so went off to a mountainside café and took up a table there spreading all her books out while the rest of us, me, my friend and his two sons hitched a ride on the ski lifts halfway up the mountain.

As we reached a place that was familiar to them they glided expertly to a standstill and waited for me to arrive. Much to their amusement I turned up a few minutes later being dragged by the ankle higher and higher up the mountain, spitting out mouthfuls of snow and pieces of pine tree. As soon as I eventually got myself together and emptied a few kilos of ice from my trousers, the three of them hopped back on the ski lift and said "have fun, we're off to the top of the mountain" and disappeared into the mist.

It then dawned on me that they had greatly overestimated my snowboarding abilities and assumed that I would be able to make it down the mountain alone. I had no choice but to try. So I strapped my feet into the boards bindings and stood up. Then I fell down. Then I stood up. And so the process continued for maybe half a kilometre until the slope dropped away at a very steep angle at which point I picked up some unintentional speed and managed to stay upright for another half kilometre.

I suddenly noticed that the sound my board was making was no longer a soft swooshing noise as it slid over the powdery snow, but a nasty scraping noise like dragging the back of a spade across rubble. It occurred to me that I had possibly taken a wrong turn and was on the side of a glacier. The next thing I knew, I hit a bump and went a few feet into the air, it felt like fifty feet but realistically was probably more like five, then down I slammed onto the hard ice on my back, all the wind knocked out of me. I lay there for a second just catching my breath and then struggled to bring myself into a sitting position. A huge whooshing noise approaches and an angry German shouts "Arschloch!!!" at me and disappears at lightning speed down the mountain. This happens three more times and I then start to wonder if laying in the snow and ice in a white ski jacket was such a good idea. Maybe black or fluorescent pink would have been safer.

At this point I had given my elbow and already dodgy knees such a bashing that I couldn't bend any of them and they were giving off heat like they were on fire, so I decided that it was time for a brief respite. The slope had flattened out a bit and so I glided slowly down to a café that had a very welcoming look about it. I stowed my snowboard in a sort of converted bike rack outside and went in to order my 'chocolat chaud' and an almond tart, then I went back outside and found a bench overlooking the side of the mountain and the valley below. As I sat down the sun came out and the mountains looked breathtaking. That moment alone, sipping hot chocolate and being in awe of the beauty of nature would make up for the pain I was feeling in my knees and elbow.

Tart finished and chocolate gone I collected my snowboard and managed to find what was probably a beginners route down the mountain. At the bottom and across the car park where we had initially come in I saw signs for some gentle slopes and so I headed over to them and caught a more civilised and less angry ski lift. From the top of these "baby" slopes I braced myself, packed snow into the knee section of my ski trousers to bring down the swelling and launched off, going at a good eight or nine feet a minute.

Over the next hour, I really picked up the speed, maintained my balance and felt a lot more confident about the whole process. All the time that I had been out on the mountain, I had my video camera in my pocket, and just as the afternoon light was turning into evening darkness my friends appeared and said "we're ready to go now". So I got them to wait while for the last time that day, I rather expertly caught the ski lift to the top and careened down the slope towards them going in a zig zag down the hill whilst they filmed me. So, as proof of my abilities and in order to forever gain the adoration of my children, I now have this ten second clip of me upright and moving down a slight incline on a mountain in France. Don't believe me? Search Youtube for "Tales of the Unexploded". Yes, give me a high five. Or don't.

My breakfast this morning may seem continental but whilst staying with my friends in Grenoble I actually had something resembling cornflakes every morning. Maybe it was provided to make me feel at home, or maybe the whole continental breakfast thing is just a lie to make the English feel hard done by as they stare into a bowl of air filled rice grains and imagine their French cousins chowing down on meats and pastries. Who knows.

My second trip snowboarding was a little different. I'd decided to ask a friend to go with me so that I wasn't tied to the schedules of my hosts like before. After some begging and pleading and bargaining with his wife, he was allowed. And so we set about arranging accommodation, a feat initially carried out over the phone by his wife in her best rusty French. As rusty as it was, she secured us some basic accommodation in a little hotel called L'hotel La Prairie, which may have got it's name from the fact that it was indeed a hotel stuck out in the middle of a prairie. We had a room each complete with a bath and a lavatory, or to make it sound more grand, I should say that we both had our own en suite rooms.

Initially on this trip when we arrived at Grenoble airport and headed for the Car rental desk, there was no snow and the whole idea of snowboarding seemed like a distant fantasy. The car had been booked online and all the payments made and accepted but suddenly the lady at the desk informed us that there was an additional 80 Euro charge for some daft, made up clause and that we couldn't take the car without paying it. Eventually after accepting that the lady possibly wasn't pretending not to speak English very well we got in the car and tried to make the best of the "free" map we had been given. I'm still not sure of the actual mileage to this day but I think we did about fifty miles through some unfamiliar countryside and ended up in a place called Meaudre. There we saw a grassy hill with ski lifts swinging in the wind looking all naked and unnecessary. Our hearts sank a bit as we noticed the bright, hot sunshine and the lack of snow, but still we carried on driving and searching for our hotel.

Although I had studied French in school, it was only for a year or less and was the second language choice of the school. German was the preferred option and what was thrust upon us. The French teacher, Madame Harris, did nothing to endear herself to any of us. To say she was a large lady would be putting it politely and she had the terrible habit of spitting out copious amounts of saliva when she spoke or rather shouted "Pardon?" or "Pourquoi?" with emphasis on the "P". It was like someone setting off a lawn sprinkler attached to a megaphone. However, some of the lessons must have sunk deep into my brain and stuck there, because when we had at one point decided to put away our manly pride and ask for directions, I sprang into action and confronted a passing peasant, who appeared to understand me and gave us directions, which I in turn appeared to understand and translated back to English for my trusty co-pilot. Tres bien!

The views from our windows were looking up into a forest of conifers that somehow had a grey hue to them, the sort of place you could imagine little red riding hood wandering through and the area was deathly silent too, which initially sounds like a bad thing, but in fact the peace was beautiful. After a few days there it snowed and the silence was so deep that you could actually hear the snowflakes landing. I know that seems far fetched but you had to be there to experience it.

The snowboarding, which was about 15 miles from the hotel really turned out well and we had a fantastic time pretending to be expert boarders who were just going slowly. My friend Scott, who had never done it before, picked it up really well under my expert tuition, (actually he stood for a while on the slopes, watched other snowboarders and then copied their movements and even decided to go to the top of the mountain and left me fannying around halfway down. I'm starting to see a pattern here where I get abandoned halfway up mountains.) However, his method of learning was certainly more effective than my lesson on the dry ski slope in Cardiff and paid off as he was able to do so well.

There was a lovely restaurant on the mountain and after a few hours of gliding over the piste, we would go and have something to eat. I went for the lasagne and a glass of chilled 7up. There was also a band at the bottom of the mountain near the toilets and it seemed that they started up every time someone went in, how considerate.

Back at the hotel, in the mornings breakfast was a self service affair, consisting of cereals or muesli, a variety of bread rolls and croissants, jams, ham, cheese, chocolate spread, locally made butter, coffee, hot chocolate and an attempt at tea. We would fill up our bellies each day and head off to the slopes feeling contented and carefree.

So you can see why my breakfast this morning made me think of my trips to France. Happy days.

Right then, I have some errands to run, some wood to fetch and I should be home in time for lunch.

Lunchtime:

I'm having tuna sandwiches for lunch. Easy and delicious. A flavour that has never seemed to change for me. I remember having these as a child and as a teenager. Tuna from a can, sprinkled with vinegar, salt and pepper. It's funny how a taste can take you back in time.

Unfortunately some things don't taste like they used to. As a child I would buy small sweets called sherbet pips that actually tasted of sherbet. Now if you try and buy them they are just rock hard flavourless drops of coloured sugar. Being born and raised in Bristol, it was customary to stick an extra letter "r" in and call them sher-bert pips.

The same loss of flavour has occurred in cola cubes, pineapple rock, chocolate tools, foam bananas and licorice wheels, but thankfully not in tuna sandwiches. A pint of squash joins me and is suitably quaffed.

The only downside to this lunch is that as I eat, my jaw clicks and it hurts. Maybe I should go back to the osteopath, but then I'm still emotionally scarred from the last visit and a little worried she might sit on me again.

Teatime:

I was just about to call my son for tea but then saw his face contorted in wonder as he watched an old black and white film on the television. He'd asked me in the past whether everything in the old days was in black and white. He meant in real life, not just in films, did everyone walk around looking grey and how did traffic lights work if everything was just two colours. A fair question I'm sure you'd agree, but this time, something else was puzzling his spongelike brain.

He turned, looked at me and then back at the TV. "Dad, that thing they're talking into like a telephone. What is it?" he said.

I looked at the TV "It is a telephone."

"But what's that circle thing on the front they keep winding round?"

And then it occurred to me, he had never seen a telephone with a dial on the front, in this world of push buttons and touch screens, all of which he is more than capable of using, he had never seen one of these before. We take for granted sometimes how quickly things change. Maybe one day he will have to explain to his children how he used to have to carry a mobile phone in his pocket unlike the communication implants they will have surgically placed behind their ears.

The old dial 'phones weren't without their charms though. Apart from the nerve tingling jangle of the bells inside as it rang, there were ways to manipulate the telephone system. Allow me to elaborate. When I was about fourteen or fifteen years old, I took a fancy to a girl who lived in the Welsh town of Pontypridd, the home town of Sir Tom Jones. We had met quite by chance in the Cardiff Arms Park rugby stadium and swapped telephone numbers and addresses.

As I remember it, her father was a bit of a grumpy character and didn't want to be bothered with phone calls at his house and so she would ring me from a telephone box or I would have to ring the telephone box at a certain time on a particular evening in the hope that she would be nearby. This system worked fairly well and we built up quite a rapport over the months, although I did have a few conversations with passing strangers who had heard the phone ringing and picked it up. However, my father, who closely monitored every detail of every bill, got very perturbed that the phone bill was escalating at an alarming rate and so he bought a phone lock.

This basically was a small lock that fitted into the first hole on the dial above the number one. This stopped the dial being turned and therefore prevented outgoing calls being made including calls to the emergency services. So if there had been a fire, the house may have burnt down along with the occupants but at least the phone bill would have been reasonable.

At the time, I wasn't proficient in the art of lock picking so I had to come up with another plan if I was to ring my long distance beau. Through my love of all things electronic I had discovered that the telephone network at that time worked on a pulse system. All that meant was that as you pulled the dial around to the number you wanted, for example seven, as you released the dial and it wound back to it's starting position, it would make an electrical connection seven times, or 'pulse' seven times. So you didn't actually need the dial. When you picked up the handset, two little spring loaded contacts popped up, and by pressing these the appropriate number of times, you could ring any number you wanted.

It was a bit long winded sometimes. The code for Pontypridd back then was 0443 so I had to tap ten times for the zero, then four times, another four and then three times. That was just the code. It was worth it though just to see the look of puzzlement on my dads face. So if you have children, be warned, they will probably out-fox you. Or maybe you could just reason with them and come to an amicable arrangement. Some people do that you know.

For tea tonight we are having egg, chips and peas, I also have a pint of squash.

Day 24 - Your Food Diary

Breakfast

Mid Morning

Lunchtime

Teatime

Other snacks

Day 25 - Thursday – A Kid in Scotland.

Breakfast:

The usual Thursday dash to be ready for work, drop my son at school and look handsome, so a quick bowl of cereal will have to do.

Ooh I do not like these, banana flavoured cereal. They have a strange taste that barely resembles banana and rather reminds me of those sweets called pear drops. There is some chemical in those things that makes me choke violently and leaves me gasping for air. I have no idea what it is, but there's hints of it in this cereal.

A cup of tea may make me late but I need to wash my throat. Rushing now, damn it.

Lunchtime:

As I've probably mentioned my parents shop is next to a bakery and it never ceases to amaze me how many people come in thinking we are the bakery and as soon as it dawns on them we aren't they give me the evil eye and skulk off slamming the door behind them. I mean, apart from the foot high letters on the window declaring the nature of the business, the rows and rows of tablets should give the game away. For crying out loud!

I have ham sandwiches, a pear, a bag of crisps and a chocolate mini roll. I used to eat these by the packet. It all started when one day my Nan approached me and said "I'd like to buy you a present, is there anything you want?". Looking back I imagine she was thinking along

143

the lines of some new trainers, a book, a box of chocolates or at least something you could fit in a bag. But without a moments hesitation I said "I'd like a shed please Nan". You can see the surprised look on her face in the photograph.

And sure enough, a week later, God bless my Nan, my brand new shed was delivered and my dad had to put together the sections and secure it on a concrete base. I was like a pig in you know what. My own shed!

When it was put up, we painted it the obligatory harvest gold colour and I set about filling it with all the mod cons I thought I would need, a frail wooden bench complete with a wood vice suitable for holding most things up to and including anything no bigger than an ants leg. A dartboard was positioned at one end with darts stabbed deceitfully into the bulls eye. An old green armchair was crammed through the door and set up as the throne for my new kingdom. But the most important addition at this point was a large blue holdall bag which was filled with electronics magazines, packets and packets of chocolate mini rolls and a never ending supply of cheap orangeade, and I mean cheap, from the post office where I got all the out of date sweets. This stuff must have been rejected by all the big drinks manufacturers as one swig would give you a blinding migraine and turn your pee luminous orange like you'd eaten one of those safety vests.

This became my solace on bad days, I would retreat to my shed, have three or four mini rolls all knocked back with a whole can of the orange acid. Then I would spend the next thirty minutes grimacing while my brain tried to run as far away from my mouth as possible and hid in a corner of my skull, which rather makes me sound like I have a square head. But after my trip to the osteopath, I don't any more.

During the eighties there was a lot of interest in Citizens Band radio, CB for short. This may have been due to films from the late seventies like Smokey and the bandit or maybe because it was a relatively cheap way to chat to your friends in comparison to the phone network. It seems to have died a death with the advent of smaller and better mobile phones but at the time I had my shed, it was all the rage and I had bought, for the princely sum of £10, a two channel, hand-held CB radio from a boy in school called Derek West. It had channel 14, which is the main one to which you listen to see if your buddies are on air and channel 30. If you wanted to ask if any of your CB friends were out there, you would call for them by their "handle" on channel 14. For example there was a man who apparently drove trucks and was known as "tiny trucker", someone calling themselves "Bigfoot", a woman calling herself "war widow" and some guy who I hope didn't clean his lorry very often called "dirty trucker".

I have sat and racked my brain for hours on end to remember my handle, but it seems to have escaped me or maybe was erased by the orange brain wash, but I'm sure it was something suitably inane. Maybe it was "shed boy" or "orangeade", I really don't remember.

Not many of my friends had CB's, well, actually none of my friends had CB's, not even Derek West as I had bought the only one he had, so I spent more time just listening to "war widow" flirt with "dirty trucker" than actually talking to anybody. The range of the hand-held was only about a mile and I wanted to extend it. Ideally I needed to increase the output but the next easiest thing was to put a bigger aerial on it.

Hmm, so what could I use? From my shed window I could see the ideal thing. A ten foot wooden stick that I could screw to the side of the shed giving me at least a fourteen foot elevation. So I promptly attached a new aerial to the stick, screwed it onto the shed and ran the cable inside and sorted the electronics. I have to say, I didn't really expect it to work, but sure enough the range increased and I briefly got in touch with a radio ham (amateur radio enthusiast) who patched my signal into his system, boosted it up and got me talking to a kid in Scotland.

It was interesting at the time but boring as hell for you to read. Even my Mum wasn't too interested when I had to explain to her where the ten foot washing line pole had gone.

Teatime:

As usual, on a Thursday, my wife is home before me and so gets on with making something for tea. Today as I entered the front door the smell of something cooking comes from the oven. A quick peek reveals a medley of frozen things sitting on baking trays, sinister looking smiley faces made from potato, chips that are too short and too pointy and would happily grace a vegetarian ninjas arsenal and some chicken thighs bubbling away as well.

On the hob are some peas boiling violently in a pan, spewing hot water all over the gas nozzles with a hissing sound as if they are trying to extinguish the flames themselves. You cant beat home cooking.

Apparently my wife is a little distracted because she is trying to arrange a taxi for a night out with some girl friends. I hate taxis. I have never had what I would call a good taxi journey, the drivers either talk too much, go the long way round or just smell of armpits.

When we were on holiday in Spain, spurred on by the knowledge that the international word for bus was bus, apart from in Wales where it is Bws, we took the opportunity to expand our universal vocabulary and went the whole hog. Brace yourselves for this, yes we caught a taxi, the international word for which is taxi, apart from in Wales where it's tacsi. Don't ask me how or why. The comedian Michael McIntyre has a whole routine about the incongruities of the Welsh language, well worth a listen.

The initial approach to a Spanish taxi driver is very important. It seems that the normal polite approach you might use in Britain doesn't work and more often than not is greeted by a grunt and the central locking being activated before you get the chance to open the door and get in.

The secret, we found, was to look like you were going to walk past them, and at the last minute, pounce to open a door, ideally on both sides of the car at the same time.

Once inside the taxi and having convinced the driver that it was actually his job to drive us from point A to point B, he drove us to a supermarket about ten kilometres away. So far so good, I mean, all we wanted was an egg custard tart. The driver we had for the return journey though couldn't have been more than about fourteen years old. The kind of lads lad that gives insurance brokers a shortness of breath and chest pains.

After passing the appropriately named "El lost Paradiso" for the fourth time, I started to wonder if our driver had ever been to Spain before. I am however left with a handy driving tip and indeed a compressed spine to prove it. Our driver had discovered, either on purpose or completely by accident, that if there were two speed bumps in close proximity of each other (i.e. within a quarter mile), if you hit the first one at the right speed, you could easily clear the second one, thus saving costly wear and tear on both the tyres and the road surfaces.

When we arrived back at the hotel and peeled our egg custard tart off the inside of the taxi, the driver asked me how much the fare was!? I was tempted to charge him for the cost of lengthening my spine, but I gave him what we had been charged for the outward journey. Maybe I missed a chance to haggle but I was just glad to be alive.

I think I need a beer.

Day 25 - Your Food Diary

Breakfast

Mid Morning

Lunchtime

Teatime

Other snacks

Day 26 - Friday -My 3 Inch Floating Head.

Breakfast:

I've woken up with a bit of a dry and sore throat. Judging by the way my wife has been glaring at me and the raw condition of my throat, I would say that it's a vague and distant possibility that I have been ever so gently snoring through the night. In my defence I would argue that it's hereditary or at least that some small creature has been nesting in the soft tissue at the back of my throat and made it floppy.

Usually the size and violence of my snoring is exacerbated by throwing alcohol into the equation. Cider tends to produce the loudest snoring, ranging down through lager, red wine, sherry and Martini all the way down to a quiet buzzing noise induced by whiskey or baileys. But back to my original argument of it being hereditary. I don't really recall too much snoring going on when I was a child other than on a Sunday afternoon, we would have had a roast dinner and then dad would put on radio 4 and listen to gardeners question time and fall asleep on the sofa, it was then the snoring would begin and he would end up waking himself from a drooling slumber just in time to hear the audience clapping as the show came to an end. Then Mum would come in with a cup of tea and some left over Yorkshire puddings smothered in strawberry jam. Delicious.

Some years later when I had married and moved to South Wales, Mum and dad came to stay overnight. I hadn't even considered that we might be kept awake the whole night by them snoring, but sure enough, shortly after they had gone to bed and drifted into a coma, dad started snoring, low and loud as he inhaled and then a noise like standing on an inflatable crow when he exhaled. We were shocked that he was able to make the light fittings tremble and the bedroom door which was a little loose in the frame, open and close slightly with each rumble.

Oh well, we thought, at least if we try and time our own breathing to his snoring we have a quieter moment in between.

And then Mum started. Nothing feminine or genteel here but a rasping honk like a pig being rubbed quickly up and down a corrugated iron sheet. And the most annoying part of it was the timing. As dad exhaled, Mum would inhale and fill the air with her terrible din, and then as she exhaled, dad would start up with his racket. The whole thing droned on all night like a monstrous twin engined demon.

We didn't sleep much that night.

For breakfast today I am having two pieces of wholemeal toast with jam and peanut butter and a cup of tea. Just making a mental note to myself to have this more often as it's so nice.

Lunchtime:

When I was about 10 years old I was fascinated by the thought that I could project images onto walls, ceilings and any fairly flat surface. I had saved up and bought a battery operated projector that played cartridges of film on a loop. This was the next step up from the hand-held version which you held up to your eye and wound a handle. I had a small selection of cartridges that were mainly clips from Disney films. I think it was made by a company called View Master.

I would play these films over and over and even got my grandparents to clear out their under stair cupboard so that we could all squeeze in and have a film show on a Saturday afternoon, every Saturday afternoon actually. I experimented with mirrors and lenses and found new ways to amuse myself and one day noticed that a reflected image could be reflected again in another mirror. Not an astounding fact for an adult, but as a 10 year old with a four year old sister, this conjured up a dastardly scheme.

Somehow I managed to get three good sized mirrors and set them up at such angles that my reflection could be beamed from my bedroom, down a short corridor and onto another mirror in my sisters bedroom. One night I waited until she was just falling asleep and set the mirrors in place, then with all the lights off and a desk lamp illuminating just my face I started to call her. Not in a normal voice but in a thin and distant voice. Soon she started to stir and as she opened her eyes, there, appearing to float in front of her was my three inch head (the image got smaller the further away it was) calling her name. She screamed and hid under the covers and I quickly and quietly removed and hid the mirrors and climbed back into bed just before my parents came up to see what all the fuss was. Who would have thought you could have such fun with mirrors.

For lunch today I have made tuna sandwiches with pepper and vinegar mixed in, I also have a bag of manly ridged crisps and a cup of tea.

Teatime:

I do believe I should have had a smaller lunch because tonight I have been invited out for a curry. My second one this week. There's only twelve of us going so it should be OK. It's in a little Indian Restaurant called the Chilli Inn. I've never been here before so when we arrive I'm a bit surprised to see that it's not much bigger than my living room.

Still, the smell coming from inside is very inviting and some of my friends have been here before and recommended it. So in we go to the strains of zithers and sitars playing over the music system and get welcomed by a group of men who are very eager to cater for our every need.

As it's such a small place they are not usually inclined to have groups of twelve descend upon them and apparently nearly had heart failure when my mate Richard rang them up to book the table. Nevertheless they have done their best and put some tables together in a corner near the window. Now, it would be fair to say that none of us there would fall into the category of small. The majority of us are over six feet tall and I'm sure that several of us are possibly three feet wide.

151

Unfortunately the tables appear to have been made for children or petite adults, and so we are very squashed up. I literally have no blood flowing to my armpits and when the poppadums and chutney's are served, I can only bend my arm at the elbow and lean in to get the correct distance between mouth and poppadum, but as I do this I drag the blokes either side of me down too. It's like synchronised poppadum diving.

Thankfully the people at the next table were coming to the end of their meal and as they left, the waiters added their table to ours. Suddenly we spread out, like a corset being undone, we all sighed with relief and jiggled our shoulders and biceps around to get the circulation going again. Now that our arms were free to move we could retrieve the poppadum shrapnel that had landed in our laps and in various other places in the vicinity.

In this particular establishment you can take along your own drinks, so we all reached with our freshly blood infused arms under the table and pulled out of our carrier bags an assortment of wines, beers, soft drinks, alcohol free ciders and fruit juice. The waiters, poised like panthers, saw another opportunity to afford us their serving skills and offered us wine glasses, pint glasses and enough ice cubes to sink the Titanic, and then asked if we were ready to order. We were.

I ordered onion bhaji to start, chicken tikka biriyani for main course, a peshwari naan and an extra serving of korma sauce. The bhaji's were not your usual round ball type creations but were flat like burgers or fritters. It didn't matter, they were delicious and as there was some mango chutney left over I smothered them with it.

Then when the super efficient waiters had removed our dirty dishes, hot plates were brought from the kitchen and placed in front of us. Onto this I emptied my chicken tikka biriyani and tucked in. Conversation around the table all but ceased as we sat eating in silence, mopping stray sauce up with our naan breads and drinking our various beverages. I have to admit to ordering the wrong sauce. I had ordered extra because often with large portions of biriyani you are left with a pile of rice, which is fine but sometimes a little dry, so an extra portion of sauce helps to lubricate it. However, korma sauce didn't really go with my meal, masala was what I meant to order. Never mind.

Three hours passed quickly and we chatted about work, hobbies, our families and anything else that came up. The bill came, we paid, said our goodbyes and went our separate ways. A good way to spend an evening although my stomach may not agree with me tomorrow.

Day 26 - Your Food Diary

Breakfast

Mid Morning

Lunchtime

Teatime

Other snacks

Day 27 - Saturday - Playing the Stick.

Breakfast:

Ow!! Yes, that's right, I said Ow! My stomach is killing me. I'm not sure it was the food last night but more likely to be the beer I had. I mean we're not talking liver destroying amounts of beer, but three bottles. I guess mixing them with super hot chutney and korma sauce isn't ideal, but I did enjoy last night. I'm thirsty more than anything else this morning so I will just have a cup of tea and nothing to eat. I do need a trip to the little boys room though, so please excuse me, I may be some time.

Lunchtime:

I had to pop into the local supermarket this morning to get some milk and bread and while I was in there, I noticed a packet of bratwurst sausages reduced in price as the sell by date was fast approaching, in fact, it's tomorrow. I'm still feeling full from last nights food but obviously I have to eat or I might die.

So for lunch I'm going to have some German sausages with a dollop of mustard on the side. English mustard, the stuff that clears your nostrils, not that girly French mustard with less heat than a cheap sleeping bag.

I don't often get around to buying German sausages, in fact it's been quite a while. I did go through a phase of buying them after a school trip to Aachen in Germany when I was fifteen or sixteen. It was a three day trip from Bristol, to Sheerness and then across to Vlissingen in Holland and all the way down to Aachen, Germany. Looking back, it seems a near pointless excursion as we spent about fifty-one hours on the coach so that we could get off and walk around Aachen town centre for five hours, also there was about eight hours each way on the boat.

All in all, it was a nightmare journey. None of us wanted to sleep as we knew that as soon as we did, some despicable things would be done to us by our classmates, our so-called friends. Sure enough, one boy called Ian Hayman fell asleep and awoke some time later to find a thick moustache had been drawn on him and marshmallows stuffed into his ears and nostrils. The rest of us fought off sleep as long as we could although, from time to time our heads would nod up and down as we drifted in and out of consciousness and smack into the coach window or the ashtray in the back of the next seat. Or worse still, we would dribble on our friends. Thankfully then I didn't snore like I do now.

When we arrived at our destination, the teacher, Mr Spiller, told us to be back at the same spot in five hours, which when you have been cooped up for a day and a half seems like heaven. We felt like caged animals let loose and went off to celebrate with some food. I think we all ordered bratwurst and chips because our food vocabulary was a bit limited. I'm not sure Ein Happy Meal existed back then.

Shortly after that, we divided up into smaller groups and went our separate ways. My group ended up in a department store of some kind and we were dazzled by the array of electronic hand held games that were available. The Germans seemed way ahead of us on that score, and so we bought some to take home with us and paid the hairy cashier our last few Deutsch marks.

She didn't even smile when we said a polite farewell.

Our five hours of freedom flew by, and after stocking up on sweets and drinks we boarded the coach for another day and a half of confinement. It's funny how sweets and drinks with foreign labels and names seem more exotic. I suppose it was an education for us to learn that Twix bars were called Raider in Germany.

The boredom of seeing mile after mile of autobahn was excruciating and eventually led to me and a boy named Christopher Manning sharing some earphones and listening to the radio on a walkman I had brought with me. We weren't even listening to music, just the crackles that a lightning storm was making on the long wave channel. When we got fed up of that and wondered if the electronic equipment might actually attract a lightning strike, I went back to listening to New Song by Howard Jones. Over and over again. I can't hear that song without having memories of that trip.

As we passed through different countries and got stopped at the borders, the teacher would shout for us to get our passports out and hold them up so that the armed guards that boarded the coach wouldn't shoot us in the head. The boys in particular were in awe of the pistols that were on their belts and for a brief moment the thought occurred to all of us "I wonder what would happen if we grabbed it". Thankfully none of us did.

In all this time, and despite consuming vast amounts of sandwiches, sweets, coke and crisps, I hadn't been to poo. There was a toilet buried appropriately enough in the bowels of the coach, but there was no way on earth that any of us were going to poo in front of our friends, people who had at least a small amount of respect for us. I mean, there was a door on the loo but we would have been mortified if anyone had seen us going near it. As an adult, I probably still wouldn't go to toilet on a coach as they always seem to be full of misjudged and badly aimed fragments. It's not about street cred' any more, it's all about hygiene.

The school trip coincided with a holiday that my parents had arranged and as the coach pulled up at the school to drop us off, there they were waiting to whisk me away to a camp-site in the darkest depths of Barmouth, North Wales.

After a few hours drive we arrived at what was referred to in the brochure as the beautiful and well maintained camp-site. I was more than ready now for the toilet and had a few pounds of sweets and bratwurst bearing down on my bowel. As my parents had booked out of season, the facilities at the site were closed for the winter, this included the toilet block and there was no toilet in our caravan, so for the next week, I broke out in white heads, sweats and tears and upon returning home a week later made a beeline straight to the comfort of our bathroom. What shot out of me was about forty thousand rock hard, light grey pellets that smelt like the angel of deaths trainers on a hot day. Not a bratwurst or Raider in sight.

I've never been back to Barmouth.

My second trip to Germany was a completely different story. Some friends of mine in Bristol knew a family who lived in Frankfurt and invited them to come and stay. After spending some time with them and getting to know them, they invited me to go and stay with their family in Germany. This was before the days of Easyjet so it was a British Airways flight I booked from Heathrow to Frankfurt Am Main airport. Having never been to an airport of that size it was somewhat overwhelming at sixteen years of age, to be dropped off by my parents and to make my way through all the security checks alone.

After a few hours of flying, the plane landed at Frankfurt airport and I was shocked to see that it was an even bigger place than Heathrow, but by now I was feeling like a seasoned traveller. It was a little disconcerting to see the airport security staff carrying machine guns as this time I had no teachers or school friends to use as human shields if things kicked off. My German was good enough for me to be able to find my way through the baggage area, out through passport control and on to the exits where the German family were waiting to meet me.

We drove for about twenty minutes and I was struck by how clean the streets were, no crisp packets blowing in the wind, no takeaway containers stuck to walls with curry sauce, no cigarette butts choking up the pavements. Everything was clean, tidy and orderly. Even the trees that lined the roads were uniformly trimmed and everything was in its rightful place.

The car pulled up in a clean and tidy parking bay and I was bundled out by mein hosts and taken to a block of apartments. I don't know if it's still the case, but in 1986 very few Germans owned a house, they all seemed to live in apartments, and to be fair this was a very nice one, three bedrooms, a living room, dining room, bathroom and kitchen. All decorated in a way that reminded me of so many subtitled films I had seen on TV. You know how there is something so "English" about the English countryside, there was something so "German" about the furnishings, huge wooden dressers lined with plates, brown wallpaper festooned with pictures of pine trees, the lace cushions on the high backed chairs and even a cuckoo clock screaming at us in German every

158

fifteen minutes.

I shared a room with the youngest of the family, Stefan an eleven year old who spoke pretty good English, so between us we were able to have a reasonable conversation. The eldest daughter, Ruth, was who I had met in England and she introduced me to her younger sister Deborah. The names of the mother and father escape me although I do remember that they were quiet and hospitable, a sweet and kindly couple.

That evening, I was told that we were going to a pub. As expected, this turned out to be a thoroughly German experience. Rows and rows of wooden benches were lined up and filled with fat, ruddy cheeked men dressed in Lederhosen and women showing much more cleavage than was necessary unless you were looking for a place to park a bike or hide encyclopaedias.

From a room at the back of the building, a five man band wandered amongst the tables and made their way to a small raised platform at the front, all the while squeezing their accordion's, banging an oversized drum and waiting for the sixth member of the band who it appeared was a master of playing the stick.

Yes, I said stick, because that's what it was. A stick like you would find on a tree, like you would throw to a dog, like you would burn on a camp fire. A stick. From time to time he would hit this stick with another stick, almost in time with the music. I wish I had known of this instrument when I was at school and they asked us to choose what we would most like to learn to play. I would have said "Please sir, I would like to play that ever so popular German instrument, the stick".

It seemed that the leader of the band, the stick man, didn't know all the words to the songs they were singing which apparently were traditional farming songs boasting about the raising and slaughtering of many pigs. Imagine you are an entertainer in an old folks home, you could stand there, begin playing your music and just get away with starting off a song like "We'll meet again, don't know where….." and the old dears would carry on singing until their oxygen ran out or their medication kicked in. This band did exactly the same, they would start the song and then the crowd would take over, all the while linking arms, clinking oversized glasses of alcohol and swaying from side to side.

We drank cider, we ate big fat spicy sausages and plates of stewed pickled cabbage and onions until late in the evening.

During the week I was there, Ruth, who was supposed to be looking after me, found other things to do and decided it was time to hand me over to her sister like a piece of lost property. As it happened, we had more in common anyway as we were the same age and so would stay up late into the night when everyone else had gone to bed chatting and finding out about our lives and cultures and ambitions. After one particularly long chat, we were a bit thirsty, so she said "follow me", made her way into the living room and produced a little key from inside a small ornament on the mantelpiece. It was the key to her parents drinks cupboard.

She quietly opened the cupboard door and there inside were more drinks than I had ever seen in one place, vodkas, whiskies, gins, liqueurs in every shade of the rainbow, all lined up neatly, shelf after shelf. We started on the top shelf, and sampled nearly every bottle all the way down to the bottom shelf, then went out into the shared garden and sat gazing at the stars in the clear night sky.

A little further down the street in an upstairs apartment, someone was playing "your latest trick" by Dire Straits and the saxophone solo rang out hauntingly through the night air.

The next day when we woke up and pretended not to have hangovers, I was bundled into a car and taken to Drosselgasse, a supposedly famous street in Germany. It was quaint, it was busy and it was once again, very German. Wine shops, sausage shops, shops selling leather goods and a whole string of people playing accordions. I mean for god's sake, don't they have any other instruments over there? There seems to be something very deeply rooted in the German psyche that makes them automatically link arms and sway from side to side whenever they hear a ruddy accordion. I wonder what happens if they hear someone just playing the stick.

As the accordion music took hold of and musically possessed my hosts, they linked arms with me and I was caught up in their frantic ritual as we swayed down the street with them singing songs of sausage farms and spoon makers. I have to say I was initially mortified, but nobody else in the street noticed as they were too busy doing the same thing and it quickly became a fun thing to do.

The week passed quickly and enjoyably with cycling trips along the River Rhine, picnics in Frankfurt zoo and lunches with many of their friends who were curious to see "Das Colin".

Soon it was time for me to go back home. Ruth quite happily helped me pack, Stefan kept hugging me and Deborah shed a few tears. As they had been so hospitable I left them an envelope with about a hundred Deutsch marks in to go towards the food and things they had provided me with.

At the airport, after much hugging and "auf wiedersehen's" I went and checked in at the British Airways desk. The lady asked if I wanted "rauchen oder nicht rauchen", so I went for the nicht rauchen option. It's hard to believe that smoking was allowed on flights back then, and even the non smoking section was in the middle of two smoking sections, so you got kippered anyway.

As I went through security, and set off all the metal detectors, two armed guards who thought they were extras from the Rambo movie's, closed in and with a great deal of shouting and pointing of machine guns at me, asked if I was carrying anything illegal, was I taking money out of the country, had I packed my own bags and what the hell was that smell?

The German diet had played havoc with my guts.

A third, uniformed, gun wielding thug joined us and proceeded to empty the contents of my luggage all over the floor. I ,of course, denied all knowledge of any illegal contraband, communist leanings or that there had ever been such a thing as the World Wars and then one of the security gorillas pulled a small package from my coat pocket. "Was ist das?" he screamed whilst taking aim at my brain.

"Ich weiss es nicht!" I whimpered looking down the barrel of his gun, my pupils smouldering every time his laser sight hit them, I had no idea what it was, I'd never seen it before. A small package about three inches square, wrapped in tissue paper and sealed with clear tape. Even I thought it looked suspicious. One of the gorillas pulled some latex gloves from his pocket and slipped them on. I felt my buttocks clench and my eyes widen in anticipation. They cut open the packet very carefully and there inside was the hundred Deutsch marks I had left the family. They had wrapped it up and returned it to me, thankfully with a note of explanation.

A kind gesture that could have got me a free prostate examination.

The security maniacs finally decided I was not a threat to the German people as a whole, looked for someone else to shoot and waved me on. So off I went dragging the spilt contents of my luggage, repacking it as I walked hurriedly away with my buttocks still clenched in fear.

Teatime:

Talking of buttocks being clenched, I've been a bit like that all day long, with trips to the loo having been a regular feature of my day. Our toilet roll bill will be greatly increased this week and the local sewage works may find themselves doing some overtime. Even the plug in air freshener stopped me as I passed and said "oh come on, this isn't fair."

Anyway, teatime has come far too quickly for my liking today and my wife has gone off to see an Abba tribute band in Swansea, so I am left with the task of feeding my ravenous children. I see that we have chicken breasts to use up, a packet of fresh noodles and a Chinese five spice sauce. So with the addition of a few vegetables I shall do some kind of stir fry and feed these beasts.

I still have a bottle of beer left from yesterday evening so I will finish that off as well and then we can all settle down for the evening and maybe watch a film or play Lego. I will be fine just as long as I don't move around too much and no-one squeezes me. I feel like an unexploded bomb, in fact that's what I shall call this journal, "Tales of the unexploded".

Day 27 - Your Food Diary

Breakfast

Mid Morning

Lunchtime

Teatime

Other snacks

Day 28 - Sunday -Mr Nix

Breakfast:

I read something many years ago, I think it was a journalist writing a
short article in a Sunday magazine, and he said that he felt Sundays
were for pancakes and love-making.

Having been married over twenty years you will not be surprised to
hear that I am just having pancakes today. A little drizzle of golden
syrup over them and a cup of tea. Almost the perfect start to the day.

Lunchtime:

Lunchtime is here already and I've not really achieved much of what I
intended, mainly due to the weather. It's not stopped raining all
morning. At one point when I was gazing out of the window looking up
the garden, I had the urge to snack on something pointless so I went to
root around in the cupboard like a pig looking for truffles. Not that I've
ever tried a truffle, the very idea of eating fungus seems odd to me, I
only just cope with mushrooms. Anyway, during my delving I came
across a bag of flavoured, highly coloured puffed rice grains, I don't
suppose it would do any harm to mention that they are called Rainbow
Drops. Wow, what a blast from the past. I used to buy these at
Speedwell Swimming pool after my class had been for their weekly
swim. Once again I'm amazed at how a taste can take you back all those
years.

I remember the joy of being a trendsetter and wearing the oh-so fashionable rubber verruca sock which was flesh coloured and would fill up with water. When you got out of the pool, the sock was so full that your foot appeared to be twice the normal size and there was a huge splatting noise every time you walked like the elephant man across the uncomfortably tiled floor. What with that and the knitted brown swimming trunks bedecked with cloth badges commemorating my astounding achievements in feet and inches, I looked a picture.

I'd had swimming lessons from when I was about seven or eight years old. My parents could ill afford it at the time but my mothers phobia of water and swimming made her determined that I would not suffer the same fears. In the beginning they would start us off in the nice warm and shallow learner's pool doing doggy paddle and generally making as much splash as possible whilst holding on to chunks of floating foam. Then in time we moved on to front crawl and back stroke and eventually were taken out into the main pool area. It seemed huge and without a doubt was at least 10 degrees colder than the small pool. There were diving boards too. A low down straight forward planky thing about 3 feet above the water, a medium one about 10 feet above the water and the highest one about 20 feet above the clouds.

We were encouraged, or rather made, to jump off of the lowest board and then the braver ones of us went up to the middle board and after much capitulating jumped off. Most of us went up to the top board, had a look and then decided quite quickly that it wasn't humanly possible and would be suicide to jump from that height and made our way back down the steps of shame to the accompaniment of jeering from the glue sniffers who always seemed to be in the public viewing gallery, maybe they'd glued themselves to the seats.

The whole thing wasn't helped by the fact that there were air vents at the top that the wind howled through, making it even colder up there and the eerie wind noise and drop in temperature just adding to the impression of height. When you're only four feet tall, a twenty foot drop with ice encrusted trunks seems a long way down.

Over the months and years that passed we improved our stamina and the distances we could swim were reflected in the overpriced badges and certificates that we received. I'm sure they made up some things just to fill the time, like rescuing a drowning rubber brick, or being able to swim in your pyjamas. I have yet to work out what use this is to me. Perhaps one night if I happen to be sleep walking in my pyjamas near a rubber bridge and I see one of the supporting bricks fall into the waters below, I will be able to rescue the brick and return it safely to the waiting arms of Mr and Mrs Rubber-Brick and it's worried brick siblings.

My teacher, in the early days, was an old man called Mr Nix. It could be Nicks or Knix, I don't know, but that was how his name sounded. He was a pleasant enough man but I felt that he always thought I could do better. He never said as much, but whatever I did, he would be stood there looking at me and shaking his head from side to side quite vigorously. So I tried harder and harder, I would swim faster and better and hold my breath for longer, I would dive in without leaving a single ripple, I would rescue the damn brick in record time. And yet, every time I looked to him for some smile of approval, some glimmer of recognition, he would still be stood there, shaking his head from side to side. This really got quite wearing and I got more than a little despondent.

Years later I found out that he wasn't disapproving of my efforts at all, it was just that the poor man had Parkinson's Disease. Maybe someone should have explained that to this paranoid eight year old.

The smell of roasted meat is drifting from the kitchen and it appears that today we have a roasted chicken, with all the trappings, roast potatoes, green beans, cabbage and gravy and a selection of sauces (from a jar) so I'm first in to grab the mint sauce and smother it over everything. Yum.

A glass of white wine would go down well but my wine rack is looking a bit naked at the moment. There's other drinks on there like gin, sherry, ginger wine, whisky, vodka and almond liqueur. None of them seem appropriate so I will go with a pint of squash. Cheers.

Teatime:

As usual, after a big lunch, I don't have the inclination to raid the fridge, larder or supermarket, so instead, as we are still full up, we are just going to have some soup I made a while ago and froze for just such an occasion. It's basically gammon, peas, chilli's and a little chicken stock, all blended until smooth, ooh and probably onions. I do stick onions in most things. The truth is, I can't actually remember what I put in this soup but on the lid of the freezer container I wrote "spicy ham and pea soup".

I have to say it's really tasty, and with a crusty bread roll dunked in it's perfect. I shall have to make some more of this, if only I could remember how. If I could wind the clock back, that might help. Isn't it funny how that thought crops up from time to time, I've already thought it today as my son was playing on a flight simulator. I wished my Grandad was alive just for one more day, so that I could show him how technology has moved on and the things that are possible now. He was a test pilot and flew planes out of Filton, Bristol and made sure that the engines were running well before the more well known and celebrated pilots took charge of the plane and the limelight.

He would wet his flying pants to know that from the comfort of a sofa he could sit in front of my 100" screen and fly a Mescherschmitt over the white cliffs of Dover or race a helicopter across the African Savannah's. I remember how chuffed he was when he purchased a calculator, a huge chunk of plastic with the tiniest of screens at the top with bright green figures blinking at you and huge numbers on the front. The simplest of children's toys these days has more electronic gubbins inside it than the calculator did. It's also been said that calculators nowadays have more complex electronics inside them than were on the Apollo moon missions.

Gramps was as deaf as a post, but was a dab hand at lip reading. Technically I don't think he should have ever flown but I do believe that it was this very impediment that made him as good at assessing the running of an engine as he was. It was almost like he could feel if something was running wrong, and that's probably exactly what he was doing. Feeling the hum, the vibrations, the torsions.

My nan gave me some photographs when Gramps died, and one of them is of an aircraft called Canopus. She told me that he had tested it before it went into service as a mail and passenger carrier. I have searched high and low to find some official record of this but haven't come up with anything that mentions my Grandfathers name. However, I have no reason to believe anything less, and so shown below is that photograph. I have been told that it is on the river Medway and that this was some sort of commemorative photo that was given out to a number of people so there may be other copies out there. What a pity we cant zoom in on the cockpit windows and see if Stanley's at the controls.

My mother has memories of her father telling stories of when he was airlifting people from Berlin and talking about the people he flew with. The way he would talk about them made it sound like a club for talented but naughty boys. They had nicknames for each other like "Bunny Johnson", "Goofy Whittaker" or "Chopsy Chester" and Gramps would be in fits of laughter telling Mum how Bunny Johnson had done a loop the loop in an open cockpit aeroplane and how they had lost their lunch and nearly fallen out. The aviation authorities would have a fit if they knew what had gone on. But these were a special breed of people.

Without their tomfoolery and daredevil tactics, the planes wouldn't have been tested in such rigorous and outlandish ways and I truly believe that the evolution of aircraft wouldn't be where it is today.

Gramps also told a story of Tommy "the mule" Crumpton, so called the mule as he was always kicking things, much to the annoyance of all the other mechanics in the hangar. One day Gramps set up a cardboard box right in Tommy "the mules" pathway and sure enough he kicked it out of the way. This arrangement was set up for a few days, until finally Gramps put a full sized steel anvil under the box. Along came Tommy, swung his leg, kicked the box and fractured his toes. He never kicked anything again.

After his retirement, Gramps could always be found in his workshop with his face perilously close to a home made blast furnace or grinding away at a piece of metal on his impossibly large lathe shouting "hell and damnation" every time he caught his finger or face on some unshielded lethal tool.

To see him turn a lump of steel into a working miniature petrol engine didn't really enthrall me at the time, I was more intent on burning ants into oblivion with a huge magnifying glass he had tucked away on his steel clad workbench. Looking back though, I should have paid more attention. Maybe my life and career choices could have been different if I had taken the time to leave the ants alone and watch and learn what he was doing. But then maybe the world might now be over run with ants. Who knows.

Early on in his retirement, Gramps, Stan, suffered some strokes which rendered his left arm almost useless. He tried to do the physiotherapy that the hospital had given him, a high tech' device that he had to squeeze fifty times a day, I think it had a special name like 'tennis ball' or something. This didn't work and just ended up frustrating him, so he had to adapt and sure enough he did. Even after the strokes he was able to produce small model aircraft, made from scratch, and then he moved onto model railways and model boats. He even built a large flotation tank in the garden, not a pond, you dare not call it a pond, it was most definitely a flotation tank for his remote control model boats, complete with a wind powered lighthouse.

171

As I understand it, radio control equipment was just becoming available at a price that made it accessible to the civilian market and Gramps bought some hugely expensive and heavy transmitters with all the bits to go into his boats. Before this, it was a case of just setting the rudder and running off to the other side of the water and hoping for the best. If a submerged branch or some weed tangled the rudder or knocked it off course, you would end up having to wade out and retrieve the boat as it circled endlessly much to the amusement of onlookers.

His pre-radio control aeroplanes were of a similar random nature too and could either circle like drunken eagles or just head straight into a clump of thorns, but either way they would always draw a crowd. I have a cine film of him, only lasting a few minutes, throwing one of his uncontrollable creations at a place called Rodway Common, Bristol, nearly forty years ago. You can see this for yourself on YouTube by searching for "Tales of the Unexploded".

Even though this kept him occupied, you could see in his eyes that he missed making full sized engines and the thrill of dipping in and out of the clouds in a flying machine that may or may not make it.

The sad thing is that my children never got to meet him. Even though it would be lovely to have him back for a day, I don't think it would be long enough. Do you?

Day 28 - Your Food Diary

Breakfast

Mid Morning

Lunchtime

Teatime

Other snacks

Day 29 - Monday -You Know Who Your Friends Are.

Breakfast:

A friend of mine once said after a spell in hospital that at times like that you find out who your true friends are. I would like to add to this thought and include when you move house.

The last time we moved, we labelled boxes so that they could go to the appropriate room without the need to rummage through them. Boxes for the kitchen were imaginatively labelled "kitchen", boxes for the bathroom labelled "bathroom" and so on.

I thought it would be amusing to label one of the boxes for my bedroom with extra (and obviously untrue) information and to get a reaction from the people helping us move, so I wrote a whole list of unsavoury items ending with "general fetish equipment and lubricants" on the side. The box got delivered safely to my bedroom and placed carefully on the bed. Not a single one of my friends commented on what was written. I now worry that it says more about me than them.

The move itself actually went fairly well. The sale of our house in South Wales however, didn't go so smoothly. Not because of any major problems, but because of incompetent solicitors and the stupidity of the man who bought our house. Initially he said he was buying the house for his daughter to live in, apparently that was a lie. He has been renting it out to a vile family who have made the neighbours lives hell. But, because of his lies and some other sob stories he came up with, we dropped the selling price and he promised to buy it in the February, but kept putting it off until the end of July. Not a huge problem but we had already moved to Bristol and were waiting for the money.

After we eventually exchanged contracts, we had a letter from the buyer's solicitor. For the purposes of this rant, the buyer shall be known as Mr Twanny.

Mr Twanny's solicitor had been instructed to get some money back from us to compensate his client for the removal of rubbish and goods left behind by us. This was total nonsense and my reply, via our solicitor, went something like this:

"The first and most disturbing point is the failure of Mr Twanny's solicitor to get my name right. On more than one occasion I have been referred to as Mr Penny. If Mr Twanny's solicitor cannot get something as basic as my name right, what hope is there of sorting out anything else or what credence can be given to any other points that have been raised?

Second. It has been stated that wardrobes had been left in the property, along with a dining table and a washing machine. The wardrobes in the bedroom are called "built in" wardrobes, which rather unsurprisingly refers to the fact that they are "built in" and therefore irremovable and constitute a feature of the property that is to remain in place until such time that the new owner decides they are not to his liking.

Third. If Mr Twanny has found a dining table at the property, then I would suggest that it is indeed a magic dining table and should be used very carefully as no such table was left by us. Our dining table is alive and well and living with us at our new address.

The washing machine too could be from the very same magical place that the imaginary dining table came from. However, the gap (which coincidently is the same size as a washing machine) between the built in dishwasher and the wall in the kitchen should give a very good indication that the washing machine is actually absent from the place it used to be and therefore <u>NOT THERE!</u>

Fourth. Mr Twanny's solicitor states that his client, Mr Twanny, is to be charged £500 for a skip to remove rubbish left by us. I would assume at this price that it is a luxury, gold lined skip and will be delivered on a bed of rose petals. My own research shows that a skip from Bob Jones in Tonyrefail will cost £90 and if someone was hired to remove the imaginary items it would cost sixty imaginary pounds."

I then went on to list my expenses incurred by Mr Twanny's fooling around and delaying tactics and sent back a counter claim. We never heard anything back.

Nothing's ever straightforward is it? Today, breakfast will be though, it's going to be two pieces of toast with thick cut marmalade and a cup of tea. Not hugely inspiring, but quite tasty and easy to do. The marmalade gives me a little flashback to teatimes at my Nan's house when my Grandfather Stan was alive, every day without fail at 4pm, they would have bread and jam (although it was marmalade, Robinsons, when they were used to have golliwogs on the jars), some cakes Nan had made and a milky coffee. I have yet to ever have a milky coffee that tastes better than the ones Nan used to make.

I'm running a bit behind schedule today, so I need to get a move on.

Lunchtime:

I completely forgot to make anything for lunch, so today I have to pop out to the bakery and get a sandwich. I've gone for sweet chilli chicken and a bag of salt and vinegar crisps. My cup of tea tastes weird because of the sweet chilli sauce, but overall, it's a tasty snack.

I don't know if I didn't speak very clearly or maybe I was too quiet, but the lady in the bakery had to ask me three times what I wanted. I was just about to rap my knuckles on her forehead and shout "Hello, anyone in?"

It's probably me. Once in Minehead, Somerset, my son and I went into a shop to buy a spade as he had brought his metal detector along and we were heading for the beach. So, I looked around the shop for a spade, couldn't find any and went up to the cashier and said "do you sell

177

spades?"

He looked so confused and just grunted "what?"

"do you sell spades?"

"what's that?"

"you know, a spade for digging, a shovel, a digging tool, an implement for moving sand or soil, a scoop?"

A blank look crossed his face and his eyes went glassy, "I don't know what that is".

He turned and asked his colleague "do we sell a...", turning back to me, "what was it again?"

"a spade!" I said, wondering if I was going mad.

"what's it used for?" said the other man.

"oh, for goodness sake" I said, "we'll go somewhere where they speak English", and so we did and we bought a spade.

I know sometimes accents can hinder smooth communications, but these guys were as British as me, just obviously lobotomised.

There's an old man who comes into my parents shop and he appears to have no tongue. I've never asked him how or why it's missing but trying to understand him is quite difficult. Thankfully he always wants the same thing and I worked out some months ago that "a har oh huhee hees" means " a jar of honey please". Unfortunately he is now under the impression that I can understand him perfectly and so babbles on endlessly with me nodding and oohing and aahing, hopefully in the right places.

The human brain is amazing though, how it can pick out familiar sounds from a tangle of words. I remember when my daughter was little and just starting to make talking sounds. One day I'd come in from work and she was quite insistent about telling me something that had happened. I remember clearly that she said "Taya peen inna manna bassoo, aww".

Breaking it up into bits we had "Taya", this was how she would say the shortened version of her name 'Kayla'.

"Peen" was cream.

"Manna" was grandma, "bassoo" was bathroom and the "aww" sound at the end indicated she had done something naughty. So putting it all together I knew that she had done something naughty with cream in grandmas bathroom.

As it turned out, that was exactly what had happened. She had seen grandma applying some kind of anti-ugly cream to herself and thought that she would have a go when no-one was looking. Her little hands made short work of the soft squeezy tube and before long she was covered in the stuff, and so was the bathroom floor.

Kids!

Teatime:

Spaghetti bolognaise for tea with garlic bread and a Lemsip. Suddenly came over all throaty and going hot and cold, so I will sit quietly for a bit and then go to bed and hope to feel better tomorrow.

Day 29 - Your Food Diary

Breakfast

Mid Morning

Lunchtime

Teatime

Other snacks

Day 30 -Tuesday -Death in a Bottle.

Breakfast:

Well, this is day thirty and time to weigh and see what the outcome is but I'm thinking I will wait until the end of the day as that will be a full thirty days. I've heard that weighing at different times of the day can create variations in the result but I'm not too worried about ounces or grammes.

Maybe a light breakfast today will be a good idea and help the end result, although, walking down the stairs I did feel a little wobble in the chin area which is never a good sign. I've felt that before and it's led to some upsetting moments on the scales. I think I will have a small bowl of cereal and obviously a cup of tea.

Mid morning

I had to write this down as I thought it highlighted the importance of knowing what you really want when you ask for something in a shop. This morning a lady came in asking for a bottle of euthanasia.

As I understand it, euthanasia is the practice whereby you end someone's life, with their consent, to bring relief from pain and suffering caused by illnesses, disabilities or disease.

Whilst I can see how this may seem acceptable to certain people in these circumstances, we most definitely do not sell euthanasia, and certainly not in a bottle.

What the lady actually wanted was a bottle of Echinacea, which is good for your immune system, not a bottle of euthanasia, which I imagine would not be good for your immune system at all.

So get it right, and next time you need something for your immune system, read the damn label.

Lunchtime:

Pleasure is such a fleeting thing isn't it and I'm always surprised where these passing moments of glee can come from. Today, someone from the same company has rung the shop, three times, and each time they have used a different name (even though I recognised their voice) and so, each time, so have I. What a silly game.

I get great satisfaction from winding up TeleSales callers. It feels like some kind of retribution for the many hours that I have been put on hold by institutions who insist on playing "lift music" or someone doing bad Bonnie Tyler impressions down the phone to me while I get told by a smug recorded voice every fifteen seconds "your call is important to us".

My favourite wind up was about two years ago. Now, I like to think that I'm fairly good at picking out where different accents come from, but this particular caller had a twang to her voice that I just couldn't pinpoint. I know it only narrows it down to the Southern Hemisphere and my apologies in advance to anyone from these places but it was possibly a South African or New Zealand accent. The call went something like this:

"Hello Sir, my name is Jasmine from the Terminally Obtuse Insurance Company. My job today is to talk at you for a while and to ignore most of what you say."

"No thanks, I'm not interested"

"We know we can beat any other insurance company when it comes to giving value for money. Do you drive?"

"Yes, I drive but I'm not interested."

"Can I take forty five minutes of your time to give you a quote?"

"A quilt?"

"No Sir, a quote."

"Why would you want to give me a quilt?"

"No Sir, a quote for your car."

"A quilt for my car? that's just bizarre, how big is it?"

"The car?"

"No, the quilt."

"No Sir, a quote."

"My car's blue, do you have it in blue?"

"No sir, I think you misunderstand, I'm offering to give you a quote for your car."

"I know, but to be honest I don't think it feels the cold, I mean, I've had the car five years and it's never mentioned it."

She hung up.

Another favourite is to answer the call and say, "hold the line please" and then just put the phone on the table and go shopping or go to work. Also, one last tip is to just say "no" to every question they ask. They quickly get fed up.

I shall chuckle to myself now as I munch on some corned beef sandwiches dripping with red sauce. Oh, yes, pure class on a plate although the fat and calorie content is playing on my mind on this last day of the "diet". A packet of salt and vinegar crisps compliment this and one of those juicy pears. All washed down with a cup of Chai tea as we have run out of "normal" tea bags. It's actually my first ever Chai and it's very nice. I'd recommend it.

Teatime:

Well, this is the last teatime before I hesitantly step toward the scales and watch the needle roll round and round. I've just had sausage, mash and peas with thick gravy so whatever the final outcome is I should probably deduct about two pounds anyway. The pint of squash I had will add some ounces too. Maybe a trip to the loo will make a difference. We shall soon see.

Day 30 - Your Food Diary

Breakfast

Mid Morning

Lunchtime

Teatime

Other snacks

185

Conclusion

Like I said at the very beginning, this would record the results, good or bad, and so here we are at the end of day thirty. I have to say that it's all gone very quickly, and looking back over what I've written, it's been fairly uneventful.

I think it's fair to say that this hasn't been a diet in the traditional dictionary definition type way, but more of a food diary. Just out of interest I looked back over the thirty days and I have had:

46 cups of tea, 40 sandwiches/rolls, 11 bags of crisps, 5 bananas, 3 apples, 2 pears, 8 pints of squash, 1 milkshake, 2 glasses of coke, 4 glasses of wine, 4 bottles of beer, 3 pints of shandy, 12 bowls of cereal, 11 pieces of toast, 3 pancakes, 4 waffles, 1 omelette, 2 spag' bol', 2 fish and chips, 1 macaroon, 2 flapjacks, 1 pot of noodles, 1 Chinese takeaway, 4 curries, 3 naan breads, 4 chocolate biscuits, 1 portion of couscous, 1 tomato bread, 2 pasta salads, 2 poached eggs, 2 sausage and mash dinners, 2 chicken pies, 1 spag' and meatballs,1 mini roll and 5 roast dinners.

I may have miscalculated some of that and missed out things like some of the toppings I put on the toast or fillings in sandwiches, but in general, I think that's most of what I ate. When you consider that this has been over thirty days, I'm still inclined to think that it's not excessive. If you ever watch some of the TV shows where they pile up on a big table a weeks worth of food eaten by some large people, I don't think my months worth of food is that shameful.

O.K. So here's the moment of truth, time to weigh. I've just been to the loo and I'm stripped down to my boxer shorts to lighten the load even more. When I first weighed thirty days ago I was exactly eighteen stone. Today I am ….....hang on....this can't be right. I am now eighteen and a half stone. So in the last thirty days I put on half a stone. How on earth do you explain that?

Perhaps it's water retention, or by the looks of things more like cake retention. How strange. Am I disappointed? I don't know how I feel about it, it's not like I feel huge, a bit wobbly maybe and I wish I could see my jawline once more before I die. Perhaps if I lost weight off of my face my jaw wouldn't click, it could be the effects of gravity pulling it out of place or the sheer weight of the food in my mouth.

So what am I going to do about this? If I keep putting on weight at the rate of half a stone a month I could be seventy two and a half stone by the time I'm fifty. Is that even possible? I heard of a case in America where a woman got so fat she couldn't move from the sofa and over a period of time, her skin melded with the fabric of the sofa and when she needed to go to hospital, the fire department had to take down a wall and carry out the sofa with her attached into it. It gives a whole new argument in favour of having removable covers.

According to some joyous website that can predict your date of death by calculating your BMI and weight/height, I am due to die in the year 2040,
Wednesday 17th October to be precise, so that would make me seventy years old, which I don't think is a bad age. What the website doesn't take into account is heavy traffic, falling masonry, savage dogs, allergies to insect bites, a really bad dose of hay fever or angry relatives. There are literally hundreds if not thousands of things that could kill you, either in a sudden attack or over a period of time.

I read recently that you can catch tapeworm from undercooked pork or meat or even from unwashed fruit. I've never heard that before and I'm not sure how reliable this source was. It also mentioned that a hundred years ago people would actually swallow tapeworms as a way to lose weight. I think it's fair to say that I don't have one, or if I do it needs to get it's act together and start ingesting my surplus food.

They can be up to fifty feet long and live for twenty years inside you. I think I'd have to start charging rent if I had one that long. My point is that maybe I will die tomorrow, nobody knows what circumstances will befall them do they? Something could kill me quickly or something could eat away inside of me slowly but I hope to be around for a bit longer though as I have a list of jobs to do, if I don't complete them my wife will kill me.

My sister had two bikes that she wasn't using and donated them to me so I think that when the better weather comes along I might dig out my old cycling shorts, the aerodynamic glasses and fingerless cycling gloves. I may even have a wig to stand in for the permed hair I once had and force my body to pedal to the local cycle track. If I did this at least once a week I would be improving my exercise regime by at least 100%.

I think that's where the problem lies, a total lack of exercise not only allows the calories to gather in my nether regions where they link arms to the sound of accordion music singing "we shall not, we shall not be moved", but also adds to my lack of energy, enthusiasm and will to do any kind of movement.

Yes, I think I have convinced myself that cycling is the way to go. I don't fancy swimming because it's cold and wet and I'm still mentally and emotionally scarred from the verruca sock incidents of my childhood. I don't fancy badminton any more as my ageing eyes can't keep up with the shuttlecock, I can just about cope with watching the dial on the microwave going round, but a 200mph feathered thing flying past my chins will just upset me.

I hope my cycling shorts are big enough now and don't go see-through as they stretch over my immense buttocks. If they do I might look like a hippo covered in cling film which would just attract the wrong type of attention on the cycle track.

So, children, if you are reading this and I am still alive, I must be doing something right. If however I have slipped into the sleep of death or a cake induced coma, treasure all the little memories life throws at you and if necessary, write them down. The people that know me could tell if I was happy or not and to the people that didn't know me, don't fret, I probably was happy but had forgotten to tell my face. Here's where I start off a song and leave you to finish it, "we'll meet again, don't know where......"

Right then, now that you're occupied with that, where did I put that cake?

Update on the April 2011 legislation

Even now, the legislation seems unclear and no specific written guidelines have been received at the shop, but some wider research has shown that it is the manufacturers of the products themselves that will need to purchase licences for each of the formulations/tablets that are on the hit list.

We heard through one company that a licence costs about £80,000 and that's just for one product, for example milk thistle. In some ways that is an appalling amount of money but the good news for the small shops that sell it, is that they don't have to pay that amount and that the product may still be available.

Other sources are saying that the British health supplement industry has kicked up such a stink about this that the rules and regulations set up and decided by the suits in Brussels may just be ignored anyway.

To be honest, we are none the wiser. Maybe as time goes on it will become clearer. If in doubt and you are particularly interested, why don't you write to your local M.P or do an internet search for "illegal vitamins April 2011".

The initial concerns of my parents that half of their stock would become illegal seem to have been a little over estimated and so they plod on, advising and helping the local community. Building up their immune systems, repairing their joints and ligaments, lifting their libido and harmonising their hormones.

It's a tough, thankless job, but someone has to do it.

Recipes and other pointless cookery stuff

Mash Thing

You will need:
2oz of grated cheese (50g)
8 large potatoes
1 packet of smokey bacon
1 large onion
1 splash of olive oil
50ml of milk
a dollop of butter

Peel the potatoes and cut them into quarters, pop them into a pot of water and bring to the boil.

Chop the onion and bacon, add them to a pan with the olive oil and fry them together.

When the potatoes are soft (you can tell by poking a knife into them) drain any remaining water off and leave them in the pan.

Now add the milk and butter to the potatoes and some salt and pepper. Now mash them until creamy with no lumps.

Add the bacon and onion to the mash and mix in with a spoon.

Now turn the mixture into an ovenproof dish and cover the top with the grated cheese.

Bake in the oven for 20 minutes on Gas mark 5, 200°c

We always have baked beans served with this and my preference is to mix the beans into the mash, but you can do whatever you like, it's a free country.

Hot Tobago Chicken and couscous

You will need: Chicken breasts (1 per person)
Chillies (2 – 5 depending on how hot you like your food)
2 Limes
1 cup of white rum

Chop the chillies into a container big enough to hold all the chicken breasts.

Squeeze the juice of both limes into the container and then chop and add the remaining lime flesh (not the outer skin/peel).

Add the rum and mix it all together.

Put the chicken breasts into the container and mix around so that the chicken is covered in the marinade and put in the fridge for at least 4 hours or better still, overnight.

When the chicken breasts are marinaded, drain the remaining marinade into a small pan and if necessary add a touch more rum.

Pan fry the chicken until cooked through and in the meantime bring the marinade to a simmer but don't boil it. As the marinade has been in contact with the raw chicken it needs to be cooked through properly. Simmering it should reduce it a bit too. Stir it from time to time so it doesn't burn.

Put some couscous in a pan (1 cup per person) and cover with boiling water and leave to absorb the water.

When the water has all gone stir the couscous to break up any lumps and serve it onto each plate, place a chicken breast on top and pour over the hot marinade.

Serve immediately.

Omelette

You will need:
50ml milk
4-6 large eggs
100g Diced cooked ham
1 tomato chopped into small pieces
Salt and pepper to taste

Add the eggs to a jug and beat together then add all the other ingredients and mix well.

Put a non stick frying pan on the heat and pour in the mixture from the jug. Heat through until bubbles start to appear through the mixture.

Now put the pan under the grill on a medium heat and cook for 6-8 minutes.

The top of the omelette should start to rise and darken.

Turn it out onto a plate and tuck in.

Hot chicken curry (serves 2 people or 1 of me)

3 chicken breasts
Fresh Ginger about the size of your thumb
5 Cloves of garlic
50g Cashew nuts
Ground cinnamon 1Tablespoon
Ground cardamom
Coriander
Ground cumin
Ground turmeric
1 tablespoon tomato ketchup
2 bay leaves
3 cloves
1 large onion
1 tin of coconut milk
1 teaspoon chilli powder

1) Chop the ginger, garlic and cashews in a processor, add 50ml of water and blitz it to form a paste.

2) Chop the onion.

3) Heat a non stick pan and the olive oil. Put in the ground cinnamon, cardamom, coriander, cumin, turmeric and cloves and stir. If it seems a little dry, add a dash more oil.

4) After about 30 seconds add the onion and stir until it starts to turn brown and then add the paste from the processor.

5) Stir in the ketchup, chilli powder and then pour in the coconut milk.

6) Add in your chicken and cook through (at least 25 minutes)

7) Serve with rice.

Pasulj recipe (pronounced pass-ool)

This isn't something that I've eaten during the thirty days but I wanted to include it as it's a very tasty and filling dish that is cheap to make. It's a Bean stew from Eastern Europe and a friend of mine who comes from that part of the world made it for me once and I was hooked.

You will need:
Two pounds of beans (I use dried mixed beans for variety), soak them overnight.

One pound of smoked ham or smoked sausage.
Two large onions
One tablespoon of oil (vegetable or olive oil)
One level tablespoon of flour
One teaspoon paprika

1) Drain the beans into a large saucepan and add one of the large onions diced.

2) Chop the ham or sausage and add it to pan and cover with water.

3) Cook slowly in a slow cooker or on a low heat for three hours.

4) When the three hours are nearly up, in another pan, dice and fry the other onion in the oil and when it is cooked add the paprika and stir it in, then add the flour.

5) Now add this mixture to the large pot, stir it in and continue to cook for another ten minutes and then serve up with crusty bread.

Delicious. Be warned though, this can make you a bit windy but it's worth it.

www.ingramcontent.com/pod-product-compliance
Lightning Source LLC
Chambersburg PA
CBHW052000090426
42741CB00008B/1483